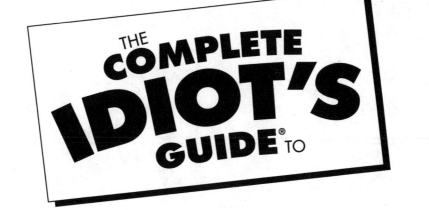

THE
COMPLETE IDIOT'S GUIDE® TO

U.S. History, Graphic Illustrated

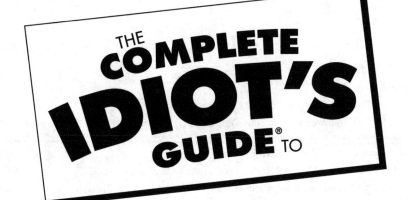

U.S. History, Graphic Illustrated

by Kenneth Hite

Illustrations by Shepherd Hendrix

A member of Penguin Group (USA) Inc.

For Harold Hite

ALPHA BOOKS

Published by the Penguin Group

Penguin Group (USA) Inc., 375 Hudson Street, New York, New York 10014, USA

Penguin Group (Canada), 90 Eglinton Avenue East, Suite 700, Toronto, Ontario M4P 2Y3, Canada (a division of Pearson Penguin Canada Inc.)

Penguin Books Ltd., 80 Strand, London WC2R 0RL, England

Penguin Ireland, 25 St. Stephen's Green, Dublin 2, Ireland (a division of Penguin Books Ltd.)

Penguin Group (Australia), 250 Camberwell Road, Camberwell, Victoria 3124, Australia (a division of Pearson Australia Group Pty. Ltd.)

Penguin Books India Pvt. Ltd., 11 Community Centre, Panchsheel Park, New Delhi—110 017, India

Penguin Group (NZ), 67 Apollo Drive, Rosedale, North Shore, Auckland 1311, New Zealand (a division of Pearson New Zealand Ltd.)

Penguin Books (South Africa) (Pty.) Ltd., 24 Sturdee Avenue, Rosebank, Johannesburg 2196, South Africa

Penguin Books Ltd., Registered Offices: 80 Strand, London WC2R 0RL, England

Note: This publication contains the opinions and ideas of its author. It is intended to provide helpful and informative material on the subject matter covered. It is sold with the understanding that the author and publisher are not engaged in rendering professional services in the book. If the reader requires personal assistance or advice, a competent professional should be consulted.

The author and publisher specifically disclaim any responsibility for any liability, loss, or risk, personal or otherwise, which is incurred as a consequence, directly or indirectly, of the use and application of any of the contents of this book.

Most Alpha books are available at special quantity discounts for bulk purchases for sales promotions, premiums, fund-raising, or educational use. Special books, or book excerpts, can also be created to fit specific needs.

For details, write: Special Markets, Alpha Books, 375 Hudson Street, New York, NY 10014.

Publisher: *Marie Butler-Knight*
Editorial Director: *Mike Sanders*
Senior Managing Editor: *Billy Fields*
Acquisitions Editor: *Karyn Gerhard*
Senior Development Editor: *Phil Kitchel*
Senior Production Editor: *Megan Douglass*

Cover/Book Designer: *Bill Thomas*
Indexer: *Brad Herriman*
Layout: *Brian Massey*
Proofreader: *John Etchison*

Contents

Foreword

Some of the folks who bought this book have skipped right over this foreword and gone on to the good stuff. Good for them, but it's of no use talking to them here.

Some of you are reading this foreword because you figure you're supposed to. You've paid for the book, it's part of the book, so you'd better take it in. To those people, I say skip it. The pictures are just a couple of pages away. A rebellion is about to start. Ben Franklin, Tecumseh, Booker T. Washington, and Edith Wilson await. Get going!

But there are some of you who are reading this foreword because you're looking for reassurance. You have your doubts. You want to read up on American history, but this? This is a big, thick comic book. Is that really appropriate? Is it respectful? Isn't history supposed to be a recitation of names, dates, and things that happened?

No. History is people. History is people doing things, and having things done to them by other people. It is stories, and it is very human stories. The names, the dates, the events are part of it, but you'll miss the story if you just look at the dry recitation. On every page of this tale there are people, brought to delightful life by the masterful pen of Shepherd Hendrix. The characters here don't each get much space, as there is a cast of hundreds and time must fly by at more than a year per page. But in a glance, each figure is made wholly human in a way that a short spurt of text or reproduction of a staid official portrait could not match. The book is informative and honest without being stilted. Kenneth Hite's script brings you the facts, but is not bereft of a point of view, nor a sense of humor.

And while you're zooming your way through over two hundred years of America, pause a moment to consider the art form in which you're reading it. Each moment is immediately brought to life, each character has a face, each event has a visible setting. The comics form makes it all comprehensible. It's not that comics are unique in this. You could make a film covering the very same content you see here. With the hundreds of locations and the hundreds of speaking rolls, such a film would not only be quite costly, it would also require the cooperation of an army of camera operators, lighting technicians, sound designers, location scouts, craft service providers, personal assistants, best boys, key grips, dolly grips, and other folks handling the most minute of efforts. This book, on the other hand, is (despite the help of a few editors and paste-up people and one foreword writer) the clear, undiluted effort of two creative souls. They bring their tone and their vision to the page without tripping over the well-meaning intent and cooperative attempts of so many others.

Comics, as a form, is thriving in an ever-growing array of uses. Like the American colonies themselves, the comics medium operated for a long time limited by the assumptions of outsiders as to what it was supposed to be. And like those colonies, once it freed itself from the limitation of those assumptions, it proved itself capable of achievement far beyond what anyone foresaw.

But forgive this fervent comics booster his digression. A story awaits you! It starts with a gunshot, ends with a victory, and in between you will find struggle, tragedy, betrayal, discovery, conflict, and wrong paths taken. Good intents will go astray, great things will be built on flawed foundations, frailties will bring down the powerful.

So turn the page. The shot is about to fired ….

—Nat Gertler
February, 2009
Which will be history by the time you read this.

Introduction

Regardless of what you may have decided in high school, there is no such thing as boring history. There are, however, an awful lot of boring historians, and an awful lot more boring history books. My great design, my big plan, my desperate hope is that *The Complete Idiot's Guide to U.S. History, Graphic Illustrated* is not one of them.

I have some aces up my sleeve here, of course. First, it's "graphically illustrated"—or as we used to say in the historical United States, it's a comic book. The comic book is an American invention, after all—an American art form, an American way to tell stories. (Yes, there were "picture-stories" in Europe before *The Yellow Kid* became the first successful American comic strip. Like millions of other Europeans, comics had to move to America to get big and successful.) Something about the always-moving rhythms of the set-up and punch line, the friendly conversation between picture and words, just *works* for American speech and story.

Second, I had the advantage of limited space. The book had to cover everything from Lexington Green in 1776 to Grant Park in 2008 in less than 200 pages, and it had to at least mention all the presidents, most of the wars, and the rest of the historical highlights. That meant I just couldn't waste any time or space boring the reader. There just wasn't room! There was always another election, or a wonderful invention, or some new upheaval to discuss on the next page—or the next panel.

In between battles and legislation, I stuck in the things we consider American—hot dogs, baseball, cowboys … and comic books. (And the things we Americans need to remember, but maybe don't want to—slavery, what happened to the Indians, riots, and James Buchanan.) Economics, the arts, industry—the American versions of all those things deserved coverage where I could find it. A few big stories demanded to be woven through the whole book: the African-American experience, the West, religion, immigration. Giving those stories some space helped, again, to keep the book from slowing down too much in any one spot.

My last big advantage, of course, is that while there is no such thing as boring history, some histories are way better than others. I got to write about the history of the United States, which—well, I'll let the least-boring American historian ever, Bernard DeVoto, tell it:

> *Sure you're romantic about American history … it is the most romantic of all histories. It began in myth and has developed through centuries of fairy stories. Whatever the time is in America it is always, at every moment, the mad and wayward hour. … If the mad, impossible voyage of Columbus or Cartier or La Salle or Coronado or John Ledyard is not romantic, if the stars did not dance in the sky when the Constitutional Convention met, if Atlantis has any landscape stranger or the other side of the moon any lights or colors or shapes more unearthly than the customary homespun of Lincoln or the morning coat of Jackson, well, I don't know what romance is. Ours is a story mad with the impossible, it is by chaos out of dream. It began as dream and it has continued as dream down to the last headline you read in a newspaper, and of our dreams there are two things above all others to be said, that only madmen could have dreamed them or would have dared to—and that we have shown a considerable faculty for making them come true.*

I just had to expand that out to fill 176 pages, and I didn't even have to draw any of it. I hope you enjoy the result. I don't think you'll be bored, at least.

Kenneth Hite
Chicago, 2009

Trademarks

PART ONE

WHEN IN THE COURSE OF HUMAN EVENTS
1775–1815

Before they voted on Lee's resolution, though, Congress decided to punch it up a bit. They appointed a committee to write a Declaration of Independence.

And the committee made their junior member do it.

Virginia congressman Thomas Jefferson was an architect, an intellectual, a planter, an inventor, and a fervent radical, who believed whole-heartedly in personal liberty.

With 187 exceptions.

He has waged cruel War against human Nature itself, violating its most sacred Rights of Life and Liberty in the Persons of a distant People who never offended him, captivating and carrying them into Slavery in another Hemisphere.

He *did* try to abolish slavery in Virginia. And he tried to condemn slavery in the Declaration of Independence.

IS "UNALIENABLE" A WORD?

Congress took that passage out, and made plenty of other changes, too.

When in the Course of human events, it becomes necessary for one people to dissolve the political bands which have connected them with another, and to assume among the powers of the earth, the separate and equal station to which the Laws of Nature and of Nature's God entitle them, a decent respect to the opinions of mankind requires that they should declare the causes which impel them to the separation. We hold these truths to be self evident, that all men are created equal, that they are endowed by their Creator with certain inalienable Rights, that among these are Life, Liberty and the pursuit of Happiness. That to secure these rights, Governments are instituted among Men, deriving their just powers from the consent of the governed, That whenever any Form of Government becomes destructive of these ends, it is the Right of the People to alter or to abolish it, and to institute new Government...

But at the end, it was still Jefferson's. And America's. And the world's.

John Hancock signed it first, on July 4, 1776, "large enough for King George to read without his spectacles."

And 55 others signed it, over the next year. Nine signers, and the son of another, would die during the war. The British imprisoned 5 signers, and 12 lost their homes. All of them risked a hangman's noose.

And for the support of this Declaration, with a firm reliance on the protection of divine Providence, we mutually pledge to each other our Lives, our Fortunes and our sacred Honor.

BRANDYWINE

GERMANTOWN

MONMOUTH

GUILFORD COURTHOSE

NINETY-SIX

EUTAW SPRINGS

The British had won (or nearly won) every battle … but every time, Washington kept his army alive to fight the next one … and the British pulled a little bit further back to New York.

In the South, American General Nathanael Greene lost (or nearly lost) every battle … but after each "win," the British were a little bit weaker … and a little bit further from their supplies.

Lord Cornwallis, the British commander, decided to march to the nearest port.

Yorktown, in Virginia.

Then the French fleet cut the British supply line.

And Washington and the French army linked up.

LAFAYETTE, THEY ARE HERE!

LITTLE FOOD, LESS AMMUNITION, AND WINTER COMING ON?

WHAT DO THEY THINK WE ARE, CONTINENTALS?

THIS TOWN IS IMPREGNABLE. WHY, IT WOULD REQUIRE A FRENCH NAVAL SQUADRON AND A MILITARY GENIUS TO TAKE IT FROM ME!

And Cornwallis was really surprised one last time. He surrendered to George Washington on October 19, 1781. The band played "The World Turned Upside Down."

The Continental Army had Yorktown, and it had the French army, but there was one thing it didn't have – money.

The Continental Congress had no power to tax, depending on voluntary contributions from the states.

WE CAN BARELY PAY OURSELVES!

The money the Congress printed, therefore, was "not worth a Continental" – by 1781, it took 186 paper dollars to equal one gold dollar.

And even when Congress did pay the troops, it was with worthless paper dollars.

THERE YOU GO, BRAVE FELLOW!

This did not endear Congress to the army.

In March of 1783, Continental officers at Newburgh, New York, proposed that Washington should either lead the army into Ohio to start their own country, or march on Congress to demand back pay, or make himself King of America and do ... anything he wanted.

THIS DREADFUL ALTERNATIVE, OF EITHER DESERTING OUR COUNTRY IN THE EXTREMEST HOUR OF HER DISTRESS OR TURNING OUR ARMS AGAINST IT ... HAS SOMETHING SO SHOCKING IN IT THAT HUMANITY REVOLTS AT THE IDEA.

Washington rejected the scheme, shamed its authors, and incidentally saved America yet again.

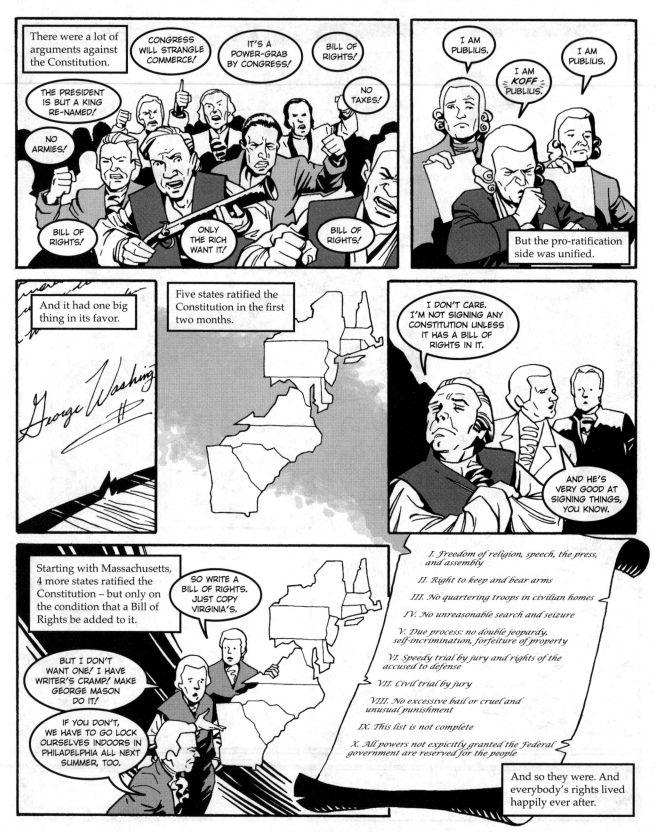

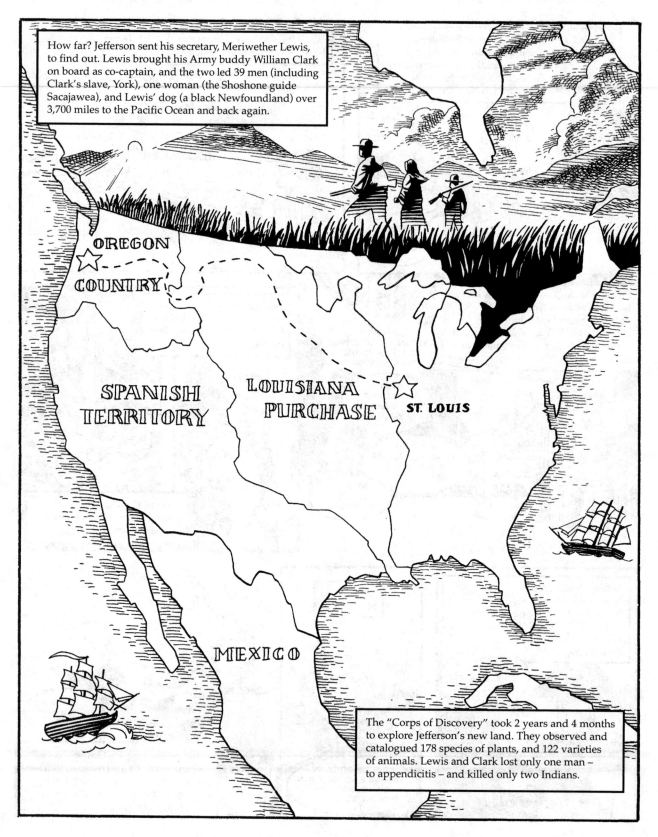

How far? Jefferson sent his secretary, Meriwether Lewis, to find out. Lewis brought his Army buddy William Clark on board as co-captain, and the two led 39 men (including Clark's slave, York), one woman (the Shoshone guide Sacajawea), and Lewis' dog (a black Newfoundland) over 3,700 miles to the Pacific Ocean and back again.

OREGON COUNTRY

SPANISH TERRITORY

LOUISIANA PURCHASE

ST. LOUIS

MEXICO

The "Corps of Discovery" took 2 years and 4 months to explore Jefferson's new land. They observed and catalogued 178 species of plants, and 122 varieties of animals. Lewis and Clark lost only one man – to appendicitis – and killed only two Indians.

The new lands brought new settlers. Farmers from Virginia and North Carolina, where tobacco was getting less profitable, tried planting cotton and sugar cane in Mississippi and Louisiana.

I DON'T KNOW ... SOMETHING'S MISSING ...

As new, more fertile lands opened up for cotton cultivation in the Deep South, so did an internal slave trade. Slave traders force-marched 10,000 or more slaves per year across the South to new plantations.

WE'VE GOT TO GO TO ALABAMA, BOYS, THE SOIL'S EXHAUSTED BACK IN VIRGINNY.

THE SOIL'S EXHAUSTED? WHAT ABOUT US?

Some got away, fleeing north to Canada or south to Indian territory in Florida.

The Constitution allowed the overseas slave trade for 20 years after ratification. In 1807, Jefferson signed a bill banning the importation of slaves.

PROTECTING DOMESTIC INDUSTRY, MISTER PRESIDENT? HOW HAMILTONIAN OF YOU.

We have the wolf by the ears, and we can neither hold him, nor safely let him go. Justice is in one scale, and self-preservation in the other.

Jefferson was tormented by the issue. He helped make sure the Northwest Territory was free soil. His writings repeatedly condemned slavery, while deprecating black intelligence and urging their deportation. Unlike Washington, he could not even free his slaves even when he died.

Jefferson's writings may even have inspired one Virginia slave rebellion, that of Gabriel Prosser in 1800.

JEFFERSON SAYS IF HE WINS THE ELECTION, HE'LL FREE THE WORKERS FROM FEDERALIST SLAVERY.

YOU THINK THAT ONE'S GOOD, YOU OUGHTA READ THE ONE ABOUT HOW "ALL MEN ARE CREATED EQUAL."

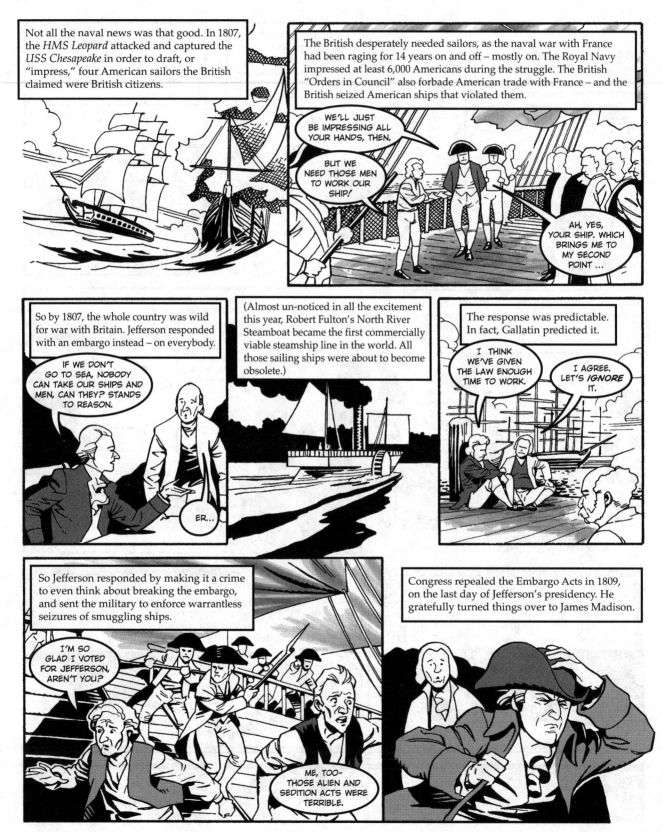

PART TWO

A HOUSE DIVIDED *1815-1865*

What sectional rivalry there was, was expressed by the Congressional Great Triumvirate: Henry Clay of Kentucky, Daniel Webster of Massachusetts, and John C. Calhoun of South Carolina.

The core policy of the Monroe administration was "The American System," which had three basic elements.

FOUR, IF YOU COUNT NAMING IT "THE AMERICAN SYSTEM."

YEA   NAY

TARIFFS
ROADS
BANKS

First, a tariff high enough to keep British goods out and support American industry. Second, national roads for internal trade. Third, a central bank to control the money supply.

In *McCulloch v. Maryland* in 1819, John Marshall ruled that the states could not regulate the Bank of the United States – the central government was supreme.

FEDERALISM ISN'T DEAD UNTIL I AM!

But states and private companies built their own "internal improvements," such as the Erie Canal …

DOES THIS TRAIN GO TO OHIO?

MA'AM, IT BARELY GOES TO *BALTIMORE.*

… and the Baltimore & Ohio Railroad. (Although when it opened in January of 1830, the track was just a mile and a half long.)

Sectional problems worked out in compromise, as with the Missouri Compromise of 1820.

MISSOURI   MAINE

SLAVE STATE FOR YOU, FREE STATE FOR YOU.

IT'S A *CORRUPT BARGAIN!*

IT'S A *GRAND COMPROMISE.*

And when the uncompromising Andrew Jackson won the most votes in 1824 – but not enough for a majority in the four-way election -- Henry Clay's control of Congress gave the presidency to John Quincy Adams.

But a new crisis was growing, as young radicals entered, and supercharged, the abolition movement. In 1831, 26-year-old William Lloyd Garrison started *The Liberator,* a newspaper that called for immediate emancipation and full citizenship for all blacks.

I WILL BE AS HARSH AS TRUTH, AND AS UNCOMPROMISING AS JUSTICE. ON THIS SUBJECT, I DO NOT WISH TO THINK, OR TO SPEAK, OR WRITE, WITH MODERATION. *NO! NO!* TELL A MAN WHOSE HOUSE IS ON FIRE TO GIVE A MODERATE ALARM ... BUT URGE ME NOT TO USE MODERATION IN A CAUSE LIKE THE PRESENT.

I AM IN EARNEST -- I WILL NOT EQUIVOCATE -- I WILL NOT EXCUSE -- I WILL NOT RETREAT A SINGLE INCH-- *AND I WILL BE HEARD.*

That same year, the preacher Nat Turner led a slave rebellion in Virginia that killed 51 whites.

WE HAVE TO PREVENT THIS HORROR FROM RECURRING.

YOU MEAN WE SHOULD FREE THE SLAVES?

NO, I MEAN WE SHOULD FORBID TEACHING THEM TO READ.

The mob response killed over 100 blacks, not including the 18 rebels hung by the state. All across the South, slave laws tightened.

Frederick Douglass violated those laws, first by teaching himself to read, and then by escaping north in 1838. In 1841, Garrison talked him into giving speeches, and Douglass became the world's best-known and most effective abolition speaker.

RIGHT IS OF NO SEX -- *TRUTH* IS OF NO COLOR-- *GOD* IS THE *FATHER* OF US ALL, AND WE ARE ALL BRETHREN.

Other slaves fled south, to the Seminole lands in Florida, and joined up with the brilliant Seminole war chief Osceola. The Seminoles kept slaves, but recruited escaped blacks as allies.

With no more than 100 warriors, Osceola held off up to 9,000 U.S. troops for two years. After his capture while under a flag of truce in 1837, the Seminole Wars continued for five more years.

I CAN'T BELIEVE YOU FELL FOR THE OLD "FAKE PEACE TALKS" TRICK.

REMIND ME AGAIN -- WHICH OF US IS THE *CIVILIZED* ONE?

Osceola was resisting Jackson's new policy of "Indian Removal."

WHAT WAS THE OLD POLICY, THEN?

The Indian Removal Act of 1830 authorized the federal government to exchange the land the Indian nations owned east of the Mississippi for new land west of the Mississippi – and to forcibly remove them if they resisted.

BUT WE'RE THE *"FIVE CIVILIZED TRIBES!"* LOOK HOW CIVILIZED WE ARE -- WE HAVE SLAVES, EVEN!

In *Worcester v. Georgia,* John Marshall tried to stall the plan by ruling that state laws had no force on Indian land. But when Jackson stared him down, Marshall blinked.

MARSHALL HAS MADE HIS RULING -- NOW LET HIM ENFORCE IT!

So it was all legal. Of about 60,000 Indians (and 2,000 slaves) relocated to Oklahoma along the "Trail of Tears," approximately 10,000 died of disease or other hardships. As Tocqueville sarcastically put it: "It is impossible to destroy men with more respect for the laws of humanity."

The *Last* of the *Mohicans*

James Fenimore Cooper

Meanwhile, 400,000 Americans wept when they read about the death of Uncas. While Andrew Jackson was closing the eastern frontier, James Fenimore Cooper was inventing the Western.

And, perhaps, the West was inventing America. The historian Frederick Jackson Turner wrote: "... that dominant individualism, working for good and for evil, and withal that buoyancy and exuberance which comes with freedom – these are traits of the frontier, or traits called out elsewhere because of the existence of the frontier."

The frontier changed America, and Americans changed the frontier, mostly into farmland. Good farmland was cheap: as low as $1.25 an acre in the Jacksonian era.

I'LL TAKE A PLUG OF TOBACCO, A BOTTLE OF WHISKEY, A POUND OF BEANS, AND AN ACRE OF PRIME FARMLAND.

THAT'S $2.65.

KEEP THE CHANGE.

Cyrus McCormick's mechanical reaper (1834) helped harvest those ever-growing farms.

John Deere's "sod-busting" steel plow (1837) tore up tough prairie soil to plant still more.

And just in case something else went wrong out West, Captain Samuel Colt's revolver (1836) was there to help.

Some farmers kept going west, even into the Mexican territory of Texas.

I DON'T LIKE HAVING ALL THESE GRINGOS IN OUR COUNTRY.

DON'T WORRY -- THEY'LL KEEP THE FRONTIER SAFE FROM AMERICAN INVASION.

DO YOU EVEN LISTEN TO THE WORDS COMING OUT OF YOUR MOUTH?

In 1835, General Santa Anna declared himself dictator of Mexico, triggering the Texas Revolution. The ruckus attracted still more American adventurers, such as former congressman Davy Crockett.

YOU ALL CAN GO TO HELL. I'M GOING TO *TEXAS.*

Santa Anna's invasion of Texas was delayed by a 13-day siege of the Alamo mission, in San Antonio. On March 6, 1836, the Alamo fell, and Santa Anna killed every one of its 183 Anglo and Tejano defenders – including Davy Crockett, Juan Seguin, and Jim Bowie.

Three weeks later, his forces killed 342 surrendered prisoners at Goliad.

Two escapees from the Goliad Massacre were present when Sam Houston captured Santa Anna with his army at San Jacinto on April 21, 1836. Texas became an independent republic.

REMEMBER THE ALAMO!!

REMEMBER GOLIAD!!

The California Gold Rush was on. In 1848, 6,000 people arrived at the diggings. In 1849, almost 90,000 "Forty-Niners" showed up – 30,000 of them from other countries. By 1852, California's non-Indian population was 250,000.

Not all of them came to mine – some, like Levi Strauss, came to sell things to the miners. His sailcloth trousers became very popular indeed.

WHAT DO YOU CALL THESE TROUSERS AGAIN?

SERGE DE NIMES WAIST-OVERALLS.

THE PANTS ARE GREAT, BUT THE NAME NEEDS WORK.

Over the next seven years, these new-minted Californians mined and refined more than 45% of the global output of gold. California gold funded a tripling of American railroad trackage, a doubling of coal production, and an increase in iron production by 12 times – almost all of it in the industrial North.

All this wealth, added to America's historically cheap land and high wages, drew 3.5 million immigrants between 1845 and 1860, mostly Germans (1.2 million) fleeing political turmoil …

I CAN'T VAIT TO DRINK AMERICAN BEER!

UND NOT VORRY ABOUT VAR ANY MORE!

… and Irish fleeing starvation. A potato famine between 1845 and 1851 killed 1 million Irish, and helped drive 1.6 million more to America.

OI THOUGHT YOU SAID WE WERE IN AMERICA.

NO IRISH NEED APPLY!

WE ARE, BUT THEY'VE SURE GOT ENGLISH SIGNS, HAVEN'T THEY?

To make things still worse, the resolute President Taylor died in office in 1850 just as the crisis hit. The next three Presidents – Millard Fillmore, Franklin Pierce, and James Buchanan – might as well have been dead in office, for all the control they exercised over the onrushing catastrophe.

WELL, I *DID* OPEN JAPAN.

In 1854, the Kansas-Nebraska Act extended "popular sovereignty" to the Kansas and Nebraska Territories. Whichever side won the election would decide whether the territories were slave or free. Radicals on both sides poured into "Bleeding Kansas" to fight it out.

The Act split the Democrats and the Whigs, and led to the creation of the anti-slavery Republican Party.

FREE MEN!

FREE SOIL!

FREMONT!

WOULD YOU ACCEPT TWO OUT OF THREE?

THE NEGRO HAS NO RIGHTS THAT THE WHITE MAN IS BOUND TO RESPECT.

In 1856, Chief Justice Roger Taney overturned the Missouri Compromise in *Dred Scott v. Sanford*.

In national speeches and a series of debates with Stephen Douglas, former congressman Lincoln raised the Republican profile across the country.

I ASK YOU, ARE YOU IN FAVOR OF CONFERRING UPON THE NEGRO THE RIGHTS AND PRIVILEGES OF CITIZENSHIP?

IN THE RIGHT TO EAT THE BREAD, WITHOUT THE LEAVE OF ANYBODY ELSE, WHICH HIS OWN HAND EARNS, HE IS MY EQUAL AND THE EQUAL OF JUDGE DOUGLAS, AND THE EQUAL OF EVERY LIVING MAN.

In 1859, a Kansas vigilante named John Brown attempted to raise a slave rebellion and seize the federal arsenal at Harper's Ferry, Virginia. He was captured by U.S. Army Lieutenant Colonel Robert E. Lee, and hanged on December 2.

"I, John Brown, am now quite certain that the crimes of this guilty land will never be purged away but with blood. I had, as I now think, vainly flattered myself that without very much bloodshed it might be done."

Hardly surprising: the North had twice the South's population.

And three times as much money.

And produced 15 times as much iron.

And built 32 times as many guns.

BUT WE GROW *KING COTTON,* SUH!

WHICH YOU CAN'T EAT, AND CAN'T SHOOT.

But the South had a lot more good generals.

The North almost had the best one, though.

IT IS WELL THAT WAR IS SO TERRIBLE -- LEST WE SHOULD GROW TOO FOND OF IT.

Colonel Robert E. Lee of Virginia was a Mexican War hero and military genius. The man who brought in John Brown, he was everyone's choice to put down the rebellion …

… until Virginia joined the Confederacy.

VIRGII

So the job went to Irvin McDowell, who had never commanded troops in combat, but was a friend of the secretary of the Treasury.

FOUR SCORE AND SEVEN YEARS AGO OUR FATHERS BROUGHT FORTH ON THIS CONTINENT A NEW NATION, CONCEIVED IN LIBERTY, AND DEDICATED TO THE PROPOSITION THAT ALL MEN ARE CREATED EQUAL.
NOW WE ARE ENGAGED IN A GREAT CIVIL WAR, TESTING WHETHER THAT NATION, OR ANY NATION, SO CONCEIVED AND SO DEDICATED, CAN LONG ENDURE. WE ARE MET ON A GREAT BATTLE-FIELD OF THAT WAR. WE HAVE COME TO DEDICATE A PORTION OF THAT FIELD, AS A FINAL RESTING PLACE FOR THOSE WHO HERE GAVE THEIR LIVES THAT THAT NATION MIGHT LIVE. IT IS ALTOGETHER FITTING AND PROPER THAT WE SHOULD DO THIS.
BUT, IN A LARGER SENSE, WE CAN NOT DEDICATE -- WE CAN NOT CONSECRATE -- WE CAN NOT HALLOW -- THIS GROUND. THE BRAVE MEN, LIVING AND DEAD, WHO STRUGGLED HERE, HAVE CONSECRATED IT, FAR ABOVE OUR POOR POWER TO ADD OR DETRACT. THE WORLD WILL LITTLE NOTE, NOR LONG REMEMBER WHAT WE SAY HERE, BUT IT CAN NEVER FORGET WHAT THEY DID HERE. IT IS FOR US THE LIVING, RATHER, TO BE DEDICATED HERE TO THE UNFINISHED WORK WHICH THEY WHO FOUGHT HERE HAVE THUS FAR SO NOBLY ADVANCED.
IT IS RATHER FOR US TO BE HERE DEDICATED TO THE GREAT TASK REMAINING BEFORE US -- THAT FROM THESE HONORED DEAD WE TAKE INCREASED DEVOTION TO THAT CAUSE FOR WHICH THEY GAVE THE LAST FULL MEASURE OF DEVOTION -- THAT WE HERE HIGHLY RESOLVE THAT THESE DEAD SHALL NOT HAVE DIED IN VAIN -- THAT THIS NATION, UNDER GOD, SHALL HAVE A NEW BIRTH OF FREEDOM -- AND THAT GOVERNMENT OF THE PEOPLE, BY THE PEOPLE, FOR THE PEOPLE, SHALL NOT PERISH FROM THE EARTH.
Lincoln made sure they didn't die in vain.

Sherman kept marching through Georgia, reached the sea, and then turned north into South Carolina.

Grant just kept the pressure on. When Sheridan's men joined Grant's forces in March, Lee was caught in a trap. He surrendered at Appomattox Court House on April 9, 1865.

The Civil War was over. 600,000 men were dead. And the South had lost.

PART THREE

YEARNING TO BREATHE FREE *1865-1898*

"Give me your tired, your poor,
Your huddled masses yearning to breathe free,
The wretched refuse of your teeming shore.
Send these, the homeless, tempest-tost to me,
I lift my lamp beside the golden door!"
— from "The New Colossus," by Emma Lazarus

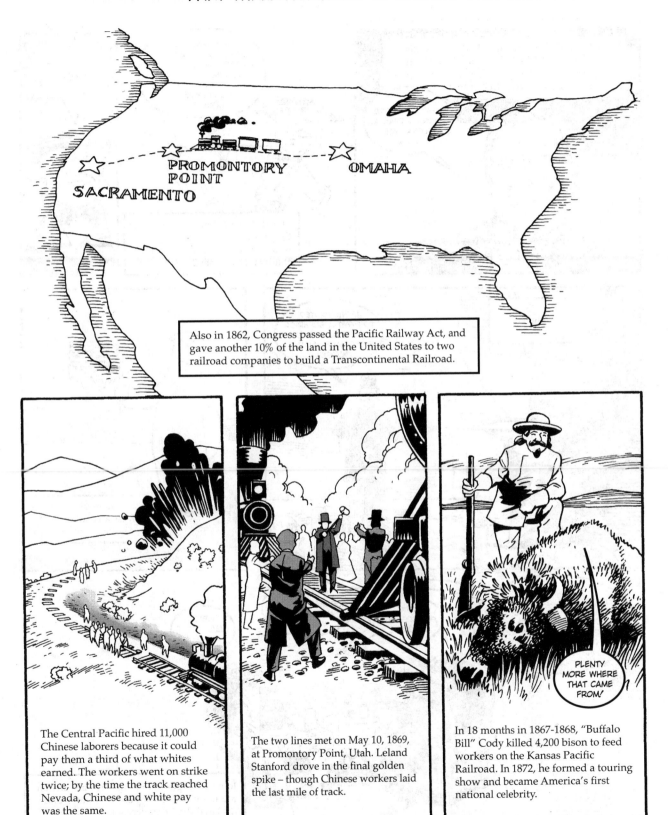

Also in 1862, Congress passed the Pacific Railway Act, and gave another 10% of the land in the United States to two railroad companies to build a Transcontinental Railroad.

The Central Pacific hired 11,000 Chinese laborers because it could pay them a third of what whites earned. The workers went on strike twice; by the time the track reached Nevada, Chinese and white pay was the same.

The two lines met on May 10, 1869, at Promontory Point, Utah. Leland Stanford drove in the final golden spike – though Chinese workers laid the last mile of track.

PLENTY MORE WHERE THAT CAME FROM!

In 18 months in 1867-1868, "Buffalo Bill" Cody killed 4,200 bison to feed workers on the Kansas Pacific Railroad. In 1872, he formed a touring show and became America's first national celebrity.

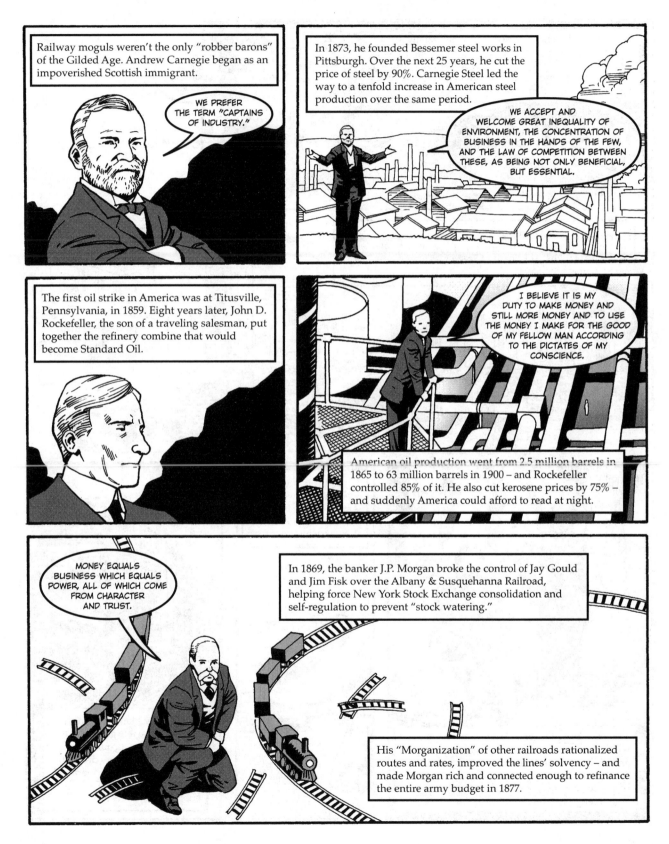

Railroads and money intersected almost literally in Chicago, which in 1865 created the world's first futures market, the Chicago Board of Trade. By 1870, the Chicago futures market purchased and sold about a quarter of the nation's grain.

BUY!

SELL!

DOES ANYONE ELSE SMELL SMOKE?

The next year, on October 8, 1871, the Great Fire hit Chicago. It killed 300 people, burnt down a third of the city, and left 100,000 homeless. The Board of Trade was open for business again two weeks later.

It's probably best not to wonder what went into America's first hot dogs, a snack pioneered on Coney Island in 1871.

WE USE EVERYTHING BUT THE SQUEAL.

The fire missed Chicago's Union Stockyards, where rival meat-packing kings Gustavus Swift and Philip Armour invented the "disassembly line" to turn cattle and hogs into meat – and into soap, glue, fertilizer, hairbrushes, buttons, knife-handles, and insulin.

By 1882, Swift and Armour had perfected the refrigerated train car. Chicago beef could reach Eastern cities already dressed, cheaper than the neighborhood butcher could sell it. The supermarket was now possible.

Since everybody knew that Grant would be re-elected in 1872, the big excitement was the candidacy of Victoria Woodhull, a stockbroker, spiritualist, and free-love advocate. She ran on the Equal Rights Party ticket with Frederick Douglass, and got perhaps 2,000 votes nationwide.

Susan B. Anthony voted for President Grant. She was arrested, convicted in circuit court without benefit of jury, and refused to pay her $100 fine.

IT WAS WE, THE PEOPLE; NOT WE, THE WHITE MALE CITIZENS; NOR YET WE, THE MALE CITIZENS; BUT WE, THE WHOLE PEOPLE, WHO FORMED THE UNION.

AND WE FORMED IT, NOT TO GIVE THE BLESSINGS OF LIBERTY, BUT TO SECURE THEM; NOT TO THE HALF OF OURSELVES AND THE HALF OF OUR POSTERITY, BUT TO THE WHOLE PEOPLE -- WOMEN AS WELL AS MEN.

Just like Congress! The construction company for the Union Pacific Railroad, Credit Mobilier, bribed 30 members of Congress (including both of Grant's vice presidents and the future president James Garfield) with shares in exchange for voting higher subsidies to the railroad. Two members were censured.

I'M EMBARRASSED TO ASSOCIATE WITH YOU, YOU PACK OF THIEVES.

Grant's private secretary was embezzling liquor taxes, the secretary of the Treasury was hiring tax farmers, the secretary of War was taking bribes from Indian agents, a U.S. attorney committed forgery, and the ambassador to Britain was selling phony mining stock.

AND PEOPLE SAY THE GOVERNMENT SHOULD REGULATE *MY* DEALINGS!

And when the over-inflated economy crashed in 1873, the Democrats regained control of the House for the first time since the Civil War.

AAAACK!

IT'S THE *PANIC* OF 1873! WHY AREN'T YOU PANICKING?

PANIC!

SELL!

IT'S GOING TO LAST SIX YEARS, SO I'M PACING MYSELF.

CLOSE THE BANK!

The United States of America celebrated its Centennial in 1876 at a grand Exhibition in Philadelphia. Like other Victorian-era World's Fairs, it included demonstrations of new inventions, including Edison's quadruplex telegraph.

Sholes and Glidden Remington typewriter

George Westinghouse's air brake

The Otis Company's steam elevator

The Emperor of Brazil received a demonstration of Alexander Graham Bell's new telephone.

QUEM E WATSON?

In 1874, Lt. Col. George Armstrong Custer discovered gold on Sioux tribal land in the Black Hills of South Dakota, and set off a gold rush of Americans panicked (and impoverished) by the Crash of 1873. Led by the shaman Sitting Bull and the warriors Gall and Crazy Horse, approximately 25,000 Sioux left the reservation.

THESE HILLS ARE *SACRED* TO US!

WELL, SINCE LAST YEAR, THEY'RE *HOLY* TO US TOO!

General George Crook set out to crush the Sioux. On June 25, 1876, Crook's subordinate Custer led his 7th Cavalry in a rash attack on a Sioux village on the Little Bighorn River.

The Sioux obliterated Custer's entire command, and the 7th Cavalry as a whole suffered 52% casualties. Sitting Bull, Gall, and a handful of Sioux escaped into Canada that winter; the U.S. Army forced the rest back onto the reservation in 1877.

In 1877, rather than go onto the reservation, Chief Joseph led 800 Nez Perce on a four-month fighting retreat toward Canada. He was intercepted by General Nelson Miles less than 40 miles from the border and surrendered on October 5.

HEAR ME, MY CHIEFS! I AM TIRED; MY HEART IS SICK AND SAD. FROM WHERE THE SUN NOW STANDS, I WILL FIGHT NO MORE FOREVER.

The last great Indian war leader, the Apache chief Geronimo, surrendered to General Miles in September 1886. He and 38 warriors had eluded 5,000 men – a quarter of the U.S. Army – for over a year. The army had been fighting the Apaches almost continuously since 1862.

I CAN'T BELIEVE YOU ACTUALLY *WANTED* THIS LAND.

On January 1, 1889, a Paiute shaman named Wovoka witnessed a solar eclipse, and announced he had a vision of a future paradise, achievable by performing the Ghost Dance. In 1890, the Ghost Dance movement spread to the Sioux reservation, where it panicked the U.S. Army into a massacre of 200 Sioux at Wounded Knee Creek.

Some of the tribes settled in Oklahoma had fought for the Confederacy, so the government confiscated their land after the Civil War. At high noon on April 22, 1889, 50,000 people raced into the former Indian Territory for the last good homestead land in the West.

WHAT ARE YOU DOING HERE?

I JUST DECIDED TO SNEAK IN A LITTLE SOONER, IS ALL.

PRIVATE PROPERTY

WHY, THAT'S *STEALING!* STEALING INDIAN TERRITORY IS ... UNNATURAL!

The next year, the Superintendent of the Census announced that "there could hardly be said to be a frontier line" remaining in the West.

By 1877, the Panic of 1873 had turned into full-fledged depression. A quarter of the railroads were out of business, and unemployment was 15%. Many who still had jobs worked half the year or less.

YOU HEAR ABOUT CUSTER? KILLED BY INJUNS BEFORE HE KNEW WHAT HIT 'IM.

LUCKY BASTARD.

On July 14, B&O Railroad workers in Martinsburg, West Virginia, learned they would be getting their second pay cut in two months. They went on strike instead, preventing trains from running on the fourth-largest railroad in the United States.

The strike spread across the Midwest – the strikers controlled the railroads and telegraph stations. Governors ordered out state militias; some fired on strikers, while others joined them. 80,000 workers were on strike across the country; half the railroad traffic in the nation was halted.

MARTINSBURG
MILWAUKEE
PITTSBURGH
ST. LOUIS   LEBANON
ALTOONA
BALTIMORE   PHILADELPHIA
CLEVELAND   BLOOMINGTON
COLUMBUS   CHICAGO   URBANA   NEWARK
CINCINNATI   DECATUR
NEW YORK   STRIKE!   BUFFALO   LOUISVILLE
PEORIA
READING

In St. Louis, strikers shut down the whole city in a general strike. For two or three days, revolution was in the air again.

ALL YOU HAVE TO DO, GENTLEMEN, FOR YOU HAVE THE NUMBERS, IS TO UNITE ON ONE IDEA -- THAT THE *WORKINGMEN* SHALL RULE THE COUNTRY.

WHAT MAN MAKES, BELONGS TO HIM, AND THE WORKINGMEN MADE THIS COUNTRY.

In late July, President Hayes ordered out federal troops. They shot no one, in many cases appearing after strike enthusiasm had waned – or been choked by "the rifle diet." Police and militia had killed 100 people, and thousands were jailed and fired.

In May of 1881, President Garfield promised his support to Clara Barton, who founded an American branch of the International Red Cross.

I FORESEE AN EMERGENCY OF A MEDICAL NATURE.

The Republicans replaced the now-tainted Hayes with the then-tainted James A. Garfield, who won a narrow victory in 1880.

Garfield served one more month until he was shot by a deranged job-seeker.

MAKE ME AMBASSADOR TO AUSTRIA! OR FRANCE. FRANCE WOULD BE GOOD.

Not coincidentally, Garfield's successor, Chester A. Arthur, signed the Pendleton Act, which set down new rules for political job-seeking.

RULE ONE: NO SHOOTING THE PRESIDENT.

Meanwhile, disgruntled job-holders were building ever larger national unions. The Knights of Labor, founded in 1867, resembled Freemasonry. Samuel Gompers' Federation of Organized Trades and Labor Unions – which became the American Federation of Labor in 1886 – resembled a tidal wave.

THERE IS NOT A RIGHT TOO LONG DENIED TO WHICH WE DO NOT ASPIRE IN ORDER TO ACHIEVE; THERE IS NOT A WRONG TOO LONG ENDURED THAT WE ARE NOT DETERMINED TO ABOLISH.

SECURITY IN OUR JOBS

NO IMMIGRANT LABOR

A FAIR DAY'S PAY FOR A FAIR DAY'S WORK

BOYCOTT UNFAIR FIRMS

Chicago was booming in another sense, as well. With its old downtown destroyed by the fire, it was ground zero for a new industrial architecture combining new powered elevators with suddenly cheaper steel frames. Architect William LeBaron Jenney built the Home Insurance Building in 1884, the first "skyscraper."

FORM EVER FOLLOWS FUNCTION. THIS IS THE LAW.

With his partner, Dankmar Adler, Chicago architect Louis Sullivan designed 90 major buildings in the next decade, reshaping the sky above America's cities.

Meanwhile, Frederick Law Olmstead, the designer of New York's Central Park (completed 1873) founded the first American landscape architecture firm in 1883.

WE WANT A GROUND TO WHICH PEOPLE MAY EASILY GO AFTER THEIR DAY'S WORK IS DONE, AND WHERE THEY MAY STROLL FOR AN HOUR, SEEING, HEARING, AND FEELING NOTHING OF THE BUSTLE AND JAR OF THE STREETS, WHERE THEY SHALL, IN EFFECT, FIND THE CITY PUT FAR AWAY FROM THEM.

Olmstead collaborated with Chicago architect Daniel Burnham to design the "White City" Columbian Exposition of 1893, a World's Fair in Chicago that spread the "City Beautiful" message to cities all across the country.

MAKE NO LITTLE PLANS. THEY HAVE NO MAGIC TO STIR MEN'S BLOOD.

Burnham designed New York's first skyscraper, the Flatiron Building, in 1902, and created the first urban growth plan, the Plan of Chicago, in 1909.

Chicago's Sears, Roebuck & Company planned big. Founded in 1886 as a mail-order watch company, by 1893 Sears sold sewing machines, plows, cream separators, clothing, and labor-saving machinery by mail at rock-bottom prices. Over a decade, Sears' Catalog circulation climbed to 3 million primarily rural customers, creating a national mass market.

MANY A SMALL THING HAS BEEN MADE LARGE BY THE RIGHT KIND OF ADVERTISING.

Mark Twain likewise sold his books by subscription and advertising; 400,000 copies by 1880. His great American novel, *Huckleberry Finn*, sold 10,000 copies a month when it was published in 1885.

Mark Twain was far from the only "national brand." From its beginnings as a patent medicine in 1886, Coca-Cola was advertised and sold in every state and territory of the Union by 1895. In 1899, Coca-Cola invented the modern franchise system by licensing bottling rights – and the right to sub-license them.

PUBLICITY, PUBLICITY, PUBLICITY IS THE GREATEST MORAL FACTOR AND FORCE IN OUR PUBLIC LIFE.

William Randolph Hearst followed the Pulitzer pattern with his *San Francisco Examiner* in 1887, and expanded his newspaper empire to five cities by 1904, and to 20 cities by 1928. America had a mass media.

With mass markets came mass newspapers. Beginning in 1882, Joseph Pulitzer kept the sales price of the *New York World* low, provided sensational crime and muck-raking stories to draw mass readership, and charged mass advertisers (such as the new department stores) to pay for it.

NEWS IS SOMETHING SOMEBODY DOESN'T WANT PRINTED; ALL ELSE IS ADVERTISING

Cleveland ordered the military to break the Pullman strike for interfering with the U.S. Mail, and filed an anti-trust injunction against the American Railway Union, calling its sympathy strike a "combination in restraint of trade."

IF IT TAKES THE ENTIRE ARMY AND NAVY OF THE UNITED STATES TO DELIVER A POSTCARD IN CHICAGO, THAT CARD WILL BE DELIVERED.

YOU'RE UNDER ARREST FOR VIOLATING THE SHERMAN ANTI-TRUST ACT.

With the strike broken, the court convicted Eugene V. Debs, head of the ARU, of violating the no-boycott injunction, and jailed him for six months.

I'M PRETTY SURE THAT'S NOT RIGHT.

YOU'LL HAVE PLENTY OF TIME TO LOOK IT UP IN JAIL, PAL.

The economic crisis also drained the government's gold reserves, which dropped from $121 million in 1893 to $9 million in February of 1895. Cleveland was forced to get J.P. Morgan to bail the Treasury out. Morgan's syndicate got U.S. gold reserves back up to $100 million by June – and made $3.5 million in profit on the transaction.

MR. MORGAN, YOU'VE SAVED THE U.S. DOLLAR!

WHICH IS A GOOD THING, AS I HAVE SO VERY MANY MORE OF THEM NOW.

Such deals drove the Democrats into a frenzy of populism. They nominated the devout William Jennings Bryan for president in 1896 on a platform of freely coined silver and renewed inflation.

WE WILL ANSWER THEIR DEMAND FOR A GOLD STANDARD BY SAYING TO THEM: YOU SHALL NOT PRESS DOWN UPON THE BROW OF LABOR THIS CROWN OF THORNS, YOU SHALL NOT CRUCIFY MANKIND UPON A CROSS OF GOLD.

The Republican nominee, William McKinley, won the votes not just of businessmen, but also Germans, factory workers, railroad workers, the middle class, and even some farmers – and the presidency.

One of McKinley's first acts was to sign a treaty annexing the "Republic" of Hawaii, a creation of sugar planters who wanted access to the U.S. market. America had taken its first irrevocable step offshore.

FROM SEA, TO SHINING SEA, TO ... WHAT?

PART FOUR

RENDEZVOUS WITH DESTINY *1898-1945*

"There is a mysterious cycle in human events. To some generations much is given. Of other generations much is expected. This generation of Americans has a rendezvous with destiny."
—Franklin Delano Roosevelt, 1936

February 15, 1898. Havana harbor.

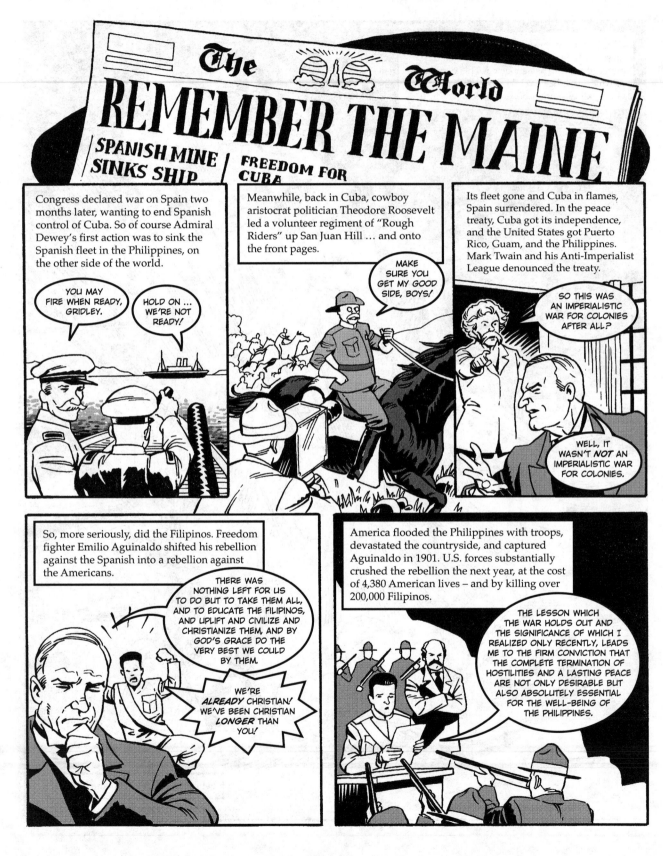

A different sort of overwhelming power was making Buffalo, New York, America's most advanced city. In 1896, George Westinghouse harnessed Niagara Falls for hydroelectricity, using the polyphase motor invented by Nikola Tesla.

Newly cheap, easily-transmitted AC electricity powered new firms in upstate New York, such as the Pittsburgh Reduction Company (eventually Alcoa), the Haloid Company (eventually Xerox), the International Time Recording Company (eventually IBM), and Acetylene Light and Power (eventually Union Carbide).

HALOID

ITR

ALCOA

UNION CARBIDE

All of this made "The City of Light" the ideal host for the Pan-American Exposition of 1901 – where an anarchist named Leon Czolgosz shot President McKinley.

McKinley's vice president, Theodore Roosevelt, became the youngest President in American history. His "Square Deal" of trust-busting and regulation departed from McKinley's domestic policy …

NO JOB DISCRIMINATION AGAINST UNIONS!

MANDATE RAILROAD RATES!

MEAT INSPECTIONS!

PURE FOOD AND DRUG ACT!

I SPEAK SOFTLY, CARRY A BIG STICK, AND IMPROVE LATIN AMERICAN BOND RATINGS!

… but his muscular "big stick" foreign policy was McKinley on steroids. The "Roosevelt Corollary" to the Monroe Doctrine pronounced that the United States could intervene in Latin America in cases of "chronic wrongdoing or impotence."

On December 17, 1903, at Kitty Hawk, North Carolina, Orville and Wilbur Wright did Nature one better. Man could fly.

The Wright Flyer was powered by gasoline. So, increasingly, was America. On January 10, 1901, an oil strike in Spindletop, Texas, tripled American oil production overnight. By the time the Wrights' Flyer III flew in 1905, the Santa Fe Railroad had gone from one oil-fired locomotive to 227.

Some 600 new oil companies sprang up in Texas alone, effectively breaking the Standard Oil monopoly. The first gas station opened in St. Louis in 1905.

With gasoline cheap and getting cheaper, a mechanic named Henry Ford took the obvious next step.

His Model T was easy to drive, rugged and reliable, and cheap to build. He sold the first ones in 1908 for a mere $850, a third the cost of other cars.

In 1913, he reversed the meat-packers' "disassembly line," and cut the time to build a Model T by 85%. A Model T now cost $550; sales increased twenty-fold.

With that, Ford decided to share the profits. In 1914, he established a $5 per day minimum salary (more than double the previous amount) and a 40-hour workweek for all Ford workers. His costs actually fell, and so did Model T prices – again. Sales increased by 150%.

Thanks to Willis Haviland Carrier, those cars could start going south. Carrier patented his "Apparatus for Treating Air" in 1906, and began air-conditioning factories, incidentally improving the quality of paint, tobacco, film, meat, and drugs.

By 1921, Carrier had invented the "centrifugal chiller," which could air-condition large indoor spaces; by 1928, the home air conditioner was practical. Business, industry, and population could move south and create the Sun Belt.

THE PLOT ISN'T MUCH, BUT THE EFFECTS ARE *TERRIFIC.*

At least one industry beat the rush to the sun. Motion pictures followed D.W. Griffith to Hollywood beginning in 1910.

HAND OVER YOUR FILM, YOU PATENT-INFRINGING VARMINT!

NO SIR. YOU CAN TELL MR. EDISON I'M GOING TO CALIFORNIA!

Another American art form was emerging in the South: New Orleans jazz. By 1910, "Jelly Roll" Morton was touring the country.

Yellow-journalistic competition between Hearst and Pulitzer drove the third new American art form of the era, comics. In 1904, its first great genius, Winsor McKay, debuted in the even yellower *New York Herald.*

MY! THIS DECADE IS CERTAINLY OCCUPYING A GREAT NUMBER OF PAGES!

But what to do? In his "Atlanta Address," delivered in 1895 to a primarily white audience, the educator Booker T. Washington called for black economic self-sufficiency, practical education, and voluntary self-segregation. Improve black peoples' lives, he preached, and leave the laws until a more propitious time.

In 1909, the sociologist W.E.B. DuBois founded, with white allies, the National Association for the Advancement of Colored People. He rejected Washington's broad-based, incrementalist position in favor of constant agitation and the education of an elite black "Talented Tenth" to carry on the political struggle.

NO RACE CAN PROSPER TILL IT LEARNS THAT THERE IS AS MUCH DIGNITY IN TILLING A FIELD AS IN WRITING A POEM. IT IS AT THE BOTTOM OF LIFE WE MUST BEGIN, AND NOT AT THE TOP.

STRIPPED OF POLITICAL POWER AND EMASCULATED BY CASTE, COLORED PEOPLE COULD NEVER GAIN SUFFICIENT ECONOMIC STRENGTH TO TAKE THEIR PLACE AS MODERN MEN.

In practical fact, neither program could be carried out in the Jim Crow South. Beginning in 1915, the black-published *Chicago Defender* newspaper began propagandizing for a "Great Migration." With the supply of immigrants cut back by WWI, Northern cities needed labor more than they needed to stay lily-white.

Life in the North, restricted to ghettos and low-wage jobs, was still harsh. But it was enough of an improvement that half a million Southern blacks came north between 1915 and 1920, and twice that in the next decade.

Wilson initially proposed "Fourteen Points" as the basis of a peace settlement in January of 1918. The Allies reacted with scorn: Clemenceau of France noted that "God only needed Ten."

I. No secret diplomacy

II. Freedom of the seas

III. Free trade

IV. Arms reductions

V. A voice for the colonies

VI. Evacuation of Russia

VII. Restore Belgium

VIII. Alsace-Lorraine to France

IX. Tyrol and Fiume to Italy

X. Democracy in Austria-Hungary

XI. Balkan readjustments

XII. Autonomy in Turkey

XIII. Independent Poland

XIV. League of Nations

By October, Wilson had secretly agreed to strip Germany of its colonies, dismember Austria-Hungary, accede to current British sea law, and demand reparations from Germany.

At the 1919 peace conference at Versailles, Wilson bargained away six more of the Points so the Allies would accede to his League of Nations.

After a terrific fight, during which Wilson suffered a debilitating stroke, Congress rejected the Versailles Treaty.

Wilson remained an invalid for the remainder of his term, his wife, Edith, essentially running the government over his forged signature.

Attorney General Palmer reacted to the chaos of 1919 by launching a series of raids; arresting 10,000 suspected anarchists, socialists, and other radicals; and eventually deporting 550 aliens without trial.

I REALLY, REALLY, *REALLY* LIKED THAT HOUSE!

Worst of all, you couldn't even drink to forget. Prohibition became the law of the land with ratification of the Eighteenth Amendment in 1920.

TAKE THAT, YOU *EYE*-TALIAN BASTARDS!

LIQUOR WASTES VALUABLE CROPS!

IT WILL ELEVATE THE RACE!

DRUNKEN MEN WILL NO LONGER ENSLAVE WOMEN!

EPHESIANS 5:18!

Prohibition was very popular … at first.

Especially among criminals, who saw a huge, lucrative national market suddenly open up. Chicago bootlegger Johnny Torrio made $30 million in five years; his successor Al Capone made perhaps $300 million.

THIS AMERICAN SYSTEM OF OURS … CALL IT AMERICANISM, CALL IT CAPITALISM, CALL IT WHAT YOU LIKE, GIVES TO EACH AND EVERY ONE OF US A GREAT OPPORTUNITY IF WE ONLY SEIZE IT WITH BOTH HANDS AND MAKE THE MOST OF IT.

For the first time, America had a national organized crime network, although it took a decade or so to get really organized.

Women's support for Prohibition had been so strong that support for women's suffrage … er … suffered.

IF WE LET 'EM VOTE, THEY'LL VOTE TO TAKE MY WHISKEY AWAY!

But in 1919, with Prohibition inevitable, Congress proposed the Nineteenth Amendment to give women the vote. The states ratified it just in time for the 1920 elections.

HERE'S TO THE LADIES! LONG MAY THEY VOTE!

IDEALLY, FOR US!

The stress of those scandals destroyed Harding's health and he died of pneumonia in 1923, making Vice President Calvin Coolidge the President.

...

Coolidge was elected in his own right the next year, not least because the economy was booming. Real per capita income increased by almost 40% in the 1920s, helped along by generous tax cuts in all brackets.

Education spending nearly doubled, too, setting the stage for a new conflict between Progressive educators and fundamentalist Christians. In 1925, William Jennings Bryan successfully prosecuted John D. Scopes for teaching human evolution in Tennessee.

SCIENCE IS A MAGNIFICENT FORCE, BUT IT IS NOT A TEACHER OF MORALS. IT CAN PERFECT MACHINERY, BUT IT ADDS NO MORAL RESTRAINTS TO PROTECT SOCIETY FROM THE MISUSE OF THE MACHINE.

Thanks in large part to Mencken, who dubbed it the "Monkey Trial," this tactical victory became a cultural defeat, and fundamentalism retreated from the political scene for 50 years.

WHAT DO YOU THINK?

I DO NOT THINK ABOUT THINGS I DON'T THINK ABOUT.

WELL, SOMETIMES.

DO YOU THINK ABOUT THINGS YOU DO THINK ABOUT?

In 1924, however, Congress decided there wasn't enough prosperity to go around, and sharply restricted immigration, especially from southern and eastern Europe. Immigration from China and Japan was banned entirely.

CLOSED. THIS MEANS YOU!

More ominously, RCA stock went from 85½ to 420 in 1928, and hit 549 the next year, when it was the most-traded stock on Wall Street despite a ludicrous price-to-earnings ratio of 73. A stock bubble was blowing up.

GIMME SOME O' THAT INTERNATIONAL COMBUSTION ENGINEERING! I HEAR IT'S THE BEE'S KNEES!

THAT'S $102 PER SHARE.

I DON'T HAVE THAT MUCH ON ME ... I'LL TAKE A HUNNERT SHARES AN' OWE YOU!

Coolidge declined to run in 1928; his technocratic secretary of Commerce, Herbert Hoover, replaced him on the Republican ticket, and won handily.

PRESIDENT COOLIDGE, WHAT ABOUT THE LONG-TERM ECONOMIC SITUATION?

WE'LL LEAVE THAT TO THE WONDER BOY.

And then came the Crash. In the week between "Black Thursday" on October 24 and "Black Tuesday" on October 29, the stock market shed $30 billion, or about the cost of World War I. By 1933, those losses would be tripled.

Hoover, of course, was crushed in the 1932 election by the Democrat Franklin D. Roosevelt, a cousin of Theodore Roosevelt. The national mood immediately brightened …

LET ME ASSERT MY BELIEF THAT THE ONLY THING WE HAVE TO FEAR IS FEAR ITSELF.

… because Prohibition was on its way to repeal, via the Twenty-first Amendment.

Twenty-first Amendment to the U.S. Constitution

Section 1: What Were We Thinking?

Section 2: No, Seriously.

Since Prohibition had been such a success, Harry Anslinger, head of the Federal Bureau of Narcotics, began pressing for a national prohibition of marijuana, which passed in 1937. America had its first "war on drugs."

But FDR had bigger fish to fry. In his first 100 days in office, Roosevelt pushed bill after bill through a special session of Congress. His "New Deal" was much more Hooverism with much better style.

THE BANKS HAVE SHUT DOWN IN *32 STATES!*

THEN SHUT THEM DOWN IN ALL *48* AND CALL IT A "BANK HOLIDAY."

THERE'S GOING TO BE A RUN ON GOLD WHEN PEOPLE FIGURE THAT OUT!

THEN WE'LL GO OFF THE GOLD STANDARD AND MAKE OWNING GOLD ILLEGAL.

YOU'RE JUST MAKING THIS UP AS YOU GO ALONG, AREN'T YOU, SIR?

He used the Dust Bowl – a severe Western drought caused by a strong La Niña effect in the Pacific from 1930 to 1938 – to help justify farm subsidies and the CCC work relief program.

I'M FROM THE GOVERNMENT-- THE PRESIDENT IS GOING TO PAY YOU NOT TO PLANT THIS YEAR.

THAT WON'T BE A CONCERN.

Roosevelt took "gas-and-water socialism" to its heights with the Tennessee Valley Authority, a network of dams and drainage projects that provided an impoverished region with subsidized electricity and flood control – at the cost of relocating 15,000 people.

DAM!

In 1935, Congress passed the Wagner Act, guaranteeing the right to organize unions, strike, and bargain collectively. FDR stayed out of a string of strikes that resulted in John L. Lewis' brand-new, harder-line Congress of Industrial Organizations growing to 2.7 million workers by 1941.

I HAVE PLEADED LABOR'S CASE, NOT IN THE QUAVERING TONES OF A FEEBLE MENDICANT ASKING ALMS, BUT IN THE THUNDERING VOICE OF THE CAPTAIN OF A MIGHTY HOST, DEMANDING THE RIGHTS TO WHICH FREE MEN ARE ENTITLED."

In 1936, Roosevelt and the Democrats won a crushing re-election victory and increased their Congressional majorities.

THAT'S *2.7* MILLION MORE WORKERS WHO'LL VOTE DEMOCRATIC NOW … HOW MANY OLD FOLKS WOULD YOU SAY THERE ARE, HARRY?

ABOUT *3.5 MILLION*?

I FEEL A *SOCIAL SECURITY* PLAN COMING ON …

With his new mandate, in 1937 FDR decided to curb the Supreme Court, which had ruled many of his New Deal programs unconstitutional.

IF YOU DON'T START LETTING THE *NEW DEAL* THROUGH, I'M GOING TO ADD SIX MORE JUSTICES.

HOW DARE YOU TRY TO BULLY THIS COURT! WE WON'T STAND FOR IT! AND ON AN ENTIRELY UNRELATED SUBJECT, YOU'LL BE PLEASED TO KNOW THAT THE COURT FINDS THE *WAGNER ACT* CONSTITUTIONAL.

But such overreaching, all those CIO strikes, and the fact that the Depression continued without much letup – unemployment in 1938 was 19% – let the Republicans come back in Congress in 1938. Allied with conservative Democrats, they could block any more Roosevelt radicalism. The New Deal was over.

Not everyone was depressed. The Roosevelt era was also the Golden Age of Hollywood.

In 1938, kids got happier, too, as the Golden Age of Comic Books began.

"Yesterday, December 7th, 1941 – a date which will live in infamy – the United States of America was suddenly and deliberately attacked by naval and air forces of the Empire of Japan."

– Franklin D. Roosevelt, December 8, 1941

The Japanese attack on the U.S. Naval base at Pearl Harbor, Hawaii, sank five ships, killed 2,402 Americans, and made Lindbergh and the isolationists irrelevant. An overconfident Hitler, allied with Japan in the Axis, declared war on the United States on December 11. The United States was at war again.

The Japanese onslaught took the Philippines, Guam, and Wake Island, and had reached the Aleutians at the tip of Alaska by June of 1942.

ALEUTIAN ISLANDS

GUAM

WAKE ISLAND

PEARL HARBOR

HAWAIIAN ISLANDS

PHILLIPPINES

The Japanese treated American P.O.W.s with utter brutality, beginning with the "Bataan Death March," a five-day ordeal during which 650 American and perhaps 10,000 Filipinos died.

President Roosevelt and California governor Earl Warren reacted by interning 48,000 Japanese aliens – and 72,000 American citizens of Japanese descent – in remote "internment camps."

YOU'RE RELOCATING THE GERMANS TOO, RIGHT?

WELL, WE'RE MOVING ADMIRAL NIMITZ AND GENERAL EISENHOWER OUT OF CALIFORNIA, IF THAT'S WHAT YOU'RE ASKING.

Racial tensions were not restricted to Japanese-Americans. The Great Migration accelerated as war industries hired more blacks; in 1943, a race riot in Detroit killed 25 blacks and 9 whites. The "zoot suit riot" in Los Angeles that year pitted sailors against Mexican-Americans.

WHY YOU BASHING ON ME, MAN?

YOU'RE DRESSED FUNNY!

YOU'RE ONE TO TALK!

American experts broke the Japanese naval code, allowing Admiral Chester Nimitz to stop the Japanese in the Battle of the Coral Sea and maul their fleet at Midway in June 1942. By August, the United States had counter-attacked, landing on Guadalcanal Island.

"The enemy now possesses a new and terrible weapon with the power to destroy many innocent lives and do incalculable damage. Should we continue to fight, not only would it result in an ultimate collapse and obliteration of the Japanese nation, but also it would lead to the total extinction of human civilization.

– Emperor Hirohito of Japan, August 14, 1945

By Truman's order, the United States dropped the first atomic bomb on Hiroshima, Japan, on August 6, 1945. America dropped the second atomic bomb on Nagasaki, Japan, on August 9, 1945. Japan surrendered five days later. Two bombs had killed 140,000 people. World War II was over, and something else had begun.

PART FIVE

TEAR DOWN THIS WALL 1945-NOW

The mass mobilizations of unionism and wartime during the 1930s and 1940s also spilled into America's arts. "Big-band" swing dominated jazz, and big-studio animation drove comics.

The Edison-style "lone inventor" was replaced by the Edison-style corporate research laboratory. Charles Carlson invented xerography in his garage in 1938; only when Haloid (later Xerox) bought, refined, and marketed it in 1948 did it succeed.

Corporate research labs brought forth the microwave oven (from Raytheon in 1945); the improved magnetic tape (from Ampex in 1946); and, most important of all, the transistor (from Bell Labs in 1947).

The mass man wanted mass consumption ...

... and paid for it with the credit card (from Diners Club in 1950).

Competition with the Communists focused new attention on the less free parts of America.

LOOK HOW AMERICA DISCRIMINATES AGAINST ITS MINORITIES! IN THE SOVIET UNION, WE KILL ALL PEOPLE EQUALLY. ESPECIALLY MINORITIES.

In 1948, Truman desegregated the U.S. military by executive order.

THE SEGREGATION STOPS HERE

A year earlier, Jackie Robinson desegregated baseball by sheer guts.

In 1948, the unpopular Truman managed to split the Democratic Party three ways. The Republicans united behind New York governor Thomas Dewey, who said as little as possible.

HE'S TOO MEAN TO THE COMMUNISTS!

HE'S TOO NICE TO THE N****S!

THE FUTURE LIES AHEAD OF US.

Truman went on a national "whistle-stop" campaign, hammering hard at the "Do-Nothing Congress."

GIVE 'EM HELL, HARRY!

I JUST TELL THE TRUTH ABOUT THEM AND THEY THINK IT'S HELL!

Nevertheless, the media thought Truman was dead in the water. Not for the first or last time, they got the story wrong.

DEWEY DEFEATS TRUMAN

But five terms of one-party rule bred corruption. Congress investigated the IRS for fixing taxes; a special prosecutor forced 166 IRS resignations or firings before Truman's attorney general fired him. Truman's military aide peddled favors for businessmen.

PSST! WANT SOME EUROPEAN PERFUME? I CAN GET IT FOR YOU CHEAP.

Congress was even more enthusiastic about investigating Communists in Truman's administration, including Soviet agents Harry Dexter White (head of the IMF), Judith Coplon (of the Justice Department), and Alger Hiss (a former State Department official) …

… and several hundred less-guilty parties. Wisconsin Senator Joseph McCarthy was particularly eager to launch headline-grabbing "investigations."

I HAVE HERE A LIST! A LIST OF 205 … ER, 57 … ER, 115 NAMES OF HIGH GOVERNMENT OFFICIALS ACTIVELY AIDING SOVIET COMMUNISM.

IS YOUR NAME ON THAT LIST, JOE?

And the "Cold War" was heating up. The Soviets blockaded the Western sectors of Berlin in 1948, but backed down after a massive American airlift supplied the city.

THIS CAN'T END WELL.

In 1949, America and Western Europe joined in the North Atlantic Treaty Organization, a defensive alliance against Soviet aggression.

IT MAY BE ENTANGLING, BUT IT FEELS SO RIGHT!

That same year, however, the Soviets detonated their own atomic bomb, and mainland China fell to the Communists.

Divinity student John Lewis ran sit-ins in Nashville; by the age of 23, he had been arrested 24 times. At 21, he helped organize – and rode in – the first Freedom Ride.

I THOUGHT I SAW DEATH, BUT NOTHING CAN MAKE ME QUESTION THE PHILOSOPHY OF NONVIOLENCE.

In 1961, the "Freedom Rides" combined the proven tactics of sitting and buses. The 436 Freedom Riders – mostly young black students – rode into segregated cities to pit Jim Crow laws at bus stations against the 1960 Supreme Court ruling requiring integration of interstate bus transportation.

THESE ANIMALS HAVE NO RESPECT FOR THE LAW.

I KNOW. AND ONCE THE KLAN FINISHES WITH THEM, I'LL GO ARREST THEM.

With a local minister, Fred Shuttlesworth, the SCLC planned a mass action in Birmingham, Alabama to boycott and protest downtown over the Easter shopping season. On Good Friday, 1963, King was arrested for violating an injunction and jailed for eight days.

Injustice anywhere is a threat to justice everywhere. We are caught in an inescapable network of mutuality, tied in a single garment of destiny. Whatever affects one directly, affects all indirectly. ... Anyone who lives inside the United States can never be considered an outsider anywhere within its bounds.

On May 2, the SCLC agreed to let 1,000 schoolchildren join protesters in marches downtown. Public Safety Commissioner "Bull" Connor met the marchers with firehoses and police dogs. But by May 10, with 2,500 protesters overfilling the jail and 3,000 more on the streets, Birmingham caved and desegregated.

The Kennedy administration was initially cool to the Movement and tried to have it both ways. But the spectacle of Birmingham – climaxing with a church bombing by the KKK in September that killed four little girls – forced Kennedy's hand.

WE SHOULD CALL MRS. KING WHILE HER HUSBAND IS IN JAIL.

WE SHOULD CALL FOR A "COOLING OFF PERIOD" AND AN END TO FREEDOM RIDES.

I'M GOING TO ORDER FEDERAL MARSHALS TO INTEGRATE THE UNIVERSITY OF MISSISSIPPI.

I'M GOING TO ORDER THE *FBI* TO WIRETAP DR. KING'S PHONE.

SO WE'RE IN AGREEMENT, THEN.

The Movement kept the pressure on Kennedy and Congress through the summer. A. Philip Randolph, the head of the Brotherhood of Pullman Sleeping Car Porters and vice president of the AFL-CIO, resurrected his 1941 plan for a vast march on Washington. His union skills and Rustin's administrative genius put together a program that allied the SCLC with the NAACP, CORE, the Urban League, and the SNCC. Eventually, 250,000 people marched.

NOTHING COUNTS BUT PRESSURE, PRESSURE, MORE PRESSURE, AND STILL MORE PRESSURE THROUGH BROAD, ORGANIZED, AGGRESSIVE MASS ACTION.

On August 28, 1963, Martin Luther King called in Lincoln's promissory note.

WE PREACH FREEDOM AROUND THE WORLD, AND WE MEAN IT, AND WE CHERISH OUR FREEDOM HERE AT HOME, BUT ARE WE TO SAY TO THE WORLD AND, MUCH MORE IMPORTANTLY, TO EACH OTHER THAT THIS IS A LAND OF THE FREE EXCEPT FOR THE NEGROES; THAT WE HAVE NO SECOND-CLASS CITIZENS EXCEPT NEGROES; THAT WE HAVE NO CLASS OR CASTE SYSTEM, NO GHETTOS, NO MASTER RACE EXCEPT WITH RESPECT TO NEGROES?

President Kennedy had finally made his own civil rights speech on June 11.

His proposed Civil Rights Act languished in Congress until his successor, President Johnson, forced it through in 1964.

SAY IT! SEGREGATION IN PUBLIC ACCOMMODATION ...

OWWW! ... AND BY STATE AND FEDERAL GOVERNMENTS ... OWW!

... AND EMPLOYMENT DISCRIMINATION ...

OWWW!... ARE ILLEGAL! OWWW!

On March 7, 1965, 600 marchers – led by John Lewis and including Rosa Parks – attempted to cross Edmund Pettus Bridge outside Selma, Alabama, on their way to Montgomery to present a petition to Governor Wallace. State troopers and county sheriffs attacked them with clubs, bullwhips, and tear gas, injuring 50 protesters.

Although the Twenty-fourth Amendment, ratified in 1964, prohibited poll taxes ...

... it was not until Johnson's Voting Rights Act in 1965 that the federal government prohibited discrimination at the voting booth, and enforced federal remedies in such cases. A century later, Reconstruction was again the law of the land.

BALLOT

TO ENSURE SERVICE

Why was this Movement successful, when previous civil rights campaigns had ultimately failed?

Part of it was the timing. The Movement started just after a war against two murderously racist empires, and just at the beginning of a new religious revival in white America.

THERE IS NO SCRIPTURAL BASIS FOR SEGREGATION. ... THE GROUND AT THE FOOT OF THE CROSS IS LEVEL, AND IT TOUCHES MY HEART WHEN I SEE WHITES STANDING SHOULDER TO SHOULDER WITH BLACKS AT THE CROSS.

Part of it was a constellation of talent and guts unprecedented in American life since the Founding Fathers.

And part of it was David Sarnoff's decision, in 1928, to fund the research of Vladimir Zworykin, and keep pouring RCA money into his invention for the next decade.

I CAN HAVE A WORKING TUBE FOR YOU IN TWO YEARS FOR $ 50,000 ... NOT INCLUDING THE $ 1,000,000 TO PAY PHILO FARNSWORTH, WHO ACTUALLY INVENTED IT LAST YEAR.

Because seeing something on television isn't the same as reading about it.

THEY'VE JUST TURNED DOGS ON THE PROTESTERS HERE IN BIRMINGHAM ... POLICE DOGS LUNGING AT PEOPLE ...

The revolution was, in fact, televised.

America's changing lifestyle churned up increasing cultural turmoil in the 1950s. Malcolm X revived black nationalism when he became the Nation of Islam's public face in 1954.

SITTING AT THE TABLE DOESN'T MAKE YOU A DINER, UNLESS YOU EAT SOME OF WHAT'S ON THAT PLATE. BEING HERE IN AMERICA DOESN'T MAKE YOU AN AMERICAN.

Miles Davis and John Coltrane revived jazz, blending bebop with melody.

Something, someone, some spirit was pursuing all of us across the desert of life and was bound to catch us before we reached heaven.

The Beat Generation tried to rebuild American letters.

John Ford looked into the abyss from the high-water mark of the Western.

THAT'LL BE THE DAY.

Television, America's newest art form, was inventing itself – from *Dragnet* to *I Love Lucy* – and rebelling against itself at the same time.

The TWILIGHT ZONE

TONIGHT ON THE NEWS: PRESIDENT EISENHOWER SENDS MORE ADVISERS TO VIETNAM.

And the blues had a baby, and they named it rock and roll.

Overseas, things were in turmoil, too. Both the United States and the Soviets tested hydrogen bombs, which ruled out open warfare between the superpowers.

So covert warfare took over. The CIA knocked over socialist governments in Iran (1953) and Guatemala (1954).

Stalin died in 1952, and the Soviets got a new leader, Nikita Khrushchev.

WE WILL BURY YOU.

In 1956, Soviet troops crushed rebellions in Poland and Hungary …

RIGHT AFTER WE FINISH BURYING EASTERN EUROPE, AGAIN.

… while the United States looked on helplessly.

AH, WHEN WE URGED EASTERN EUROPE TO RISE UP AGAINST THEIR SOVIET MASTERS, WE, ER, HAD MORE IN MIND SOMETHING ALONG THE LINES OF, AH, A STINGINGLY SATIRICAL PLAY. EVEN A SERIES OF PLAYS.

It couldn't even condemn Soviet aggression in Hungary, since its own allies – Britain, France, and Israel – invaded Egypt the same week.

YIP YIP YIP!

ARF ARF!

GROWF!!

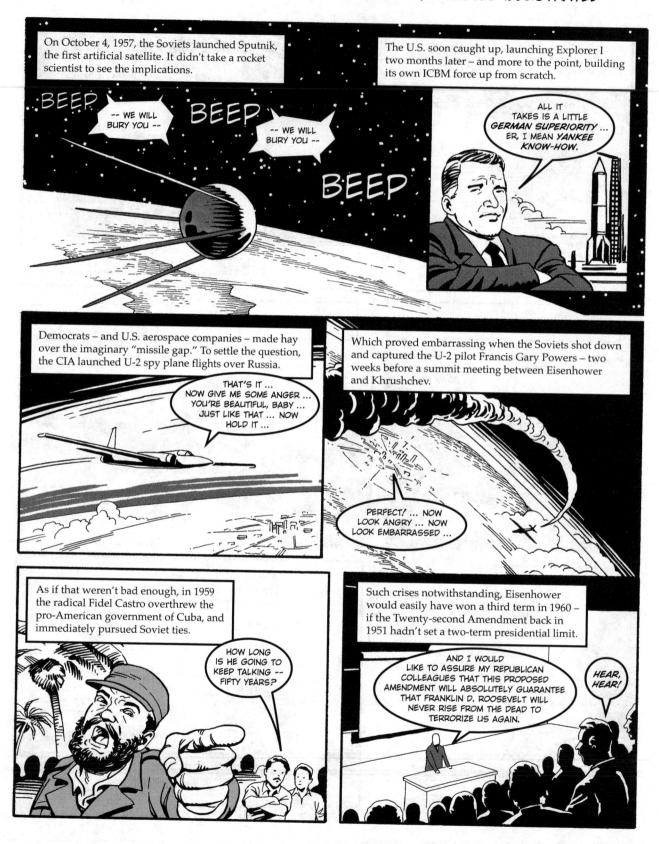

Instead, Eisenhower's vice president, Richard Nixon, ran against the Democratic senator from Massachusetts, John F. Kennedy.

Thanks to his running mate, Senator "Landslide" Lyndon Johnson of Texas – and to the Chicago machine boss Richard J. Daley – Kennedy defeated Nixon after a squeaker election.

SO THAT'S HOW THE GAME IS PLAYED, EH?

Kennedy recognized the symbolic importance of the "Space Race." After Soviet cosmonaut Yuri Gagarin became the first man in space, Kennedy doubled down.

I BELIEVE THAT THIS NATION SHOULD COMMIT ITSELF TO ACHIEVING THE GOAL, BEFORE THIS DECADE IS OUT, OF LANDING A MAN ON THE MOON AND RETURNING HIM BACK SAFELY TO THE EARTH.

NO SINGLE SPACE PROJECT IN THIS PERIOD WILL BE MORE IMPRESSIVE TO MANKIND, OR MORE IMPORTANT FOR THE LONG-RANGE EXPLORATION OF SPACE; AND NONE WILL BE SO DIFFICULT OR EXPENSIVE TO ACCOMPLISH.

The American space effort got a boost in 1958, when Jack Kilby invented the integrated circuit, or silicon chip. Suddenly payloads could be a lot smaller, and a lot smarter.

For instance, the United States launched the first communications satellite, Telstar, in 1962.

This can't end well.

JED NAMED A MAN 'BOUT STORY A LITTLE HERE'S

POOR MOUNTAINEER BARELY KEPT HIS FAMILY FED

Other parts of the future started coming true:

Theodore H. Maiman built the first working laser in 1960.

And in even better news, William House invented the cochlear implant for the deaf in 1961.

POOR MOUNTAINEER BARELY KEPT HIS FAMILY FED.

TAKE IT BACK OUT.

In April of 1961, Kennedy approved a CIA invasion of Cuba, but refused to provide U.S. air or naval support. This "Bay of Pigs" failure sealed Castro's domination of the island. By 1962, 200,000 Cubans had fled to America; another 300,000 would join them in the next decade.

A similarly embarrassing exodus from East Germany to West Berlin drove the Communists to erect the Berlin Wall in August 1961. Kennedy allowed the wall to stand, but made good propaganda from a bad situation with a fiery oration in now-isolated West Berlin.

ALL FREE MEN, WHEREVER THEY MAY LIVE, ARE CITIZENS OF BERLIN, AND, THEREFORE, AS A FREE MAN, I TAKE PRIDE IN THE WORDS "ICH BIN EIN BERLINER."

Looking for better covert warriors than the CIA, Kennedy vastly expanded the U.S. Army Special Forces, launching a PR campaign for the newly dubbed "Green Berets."

WITH THIS DEPLOYMENT, PRESIDENT KENNEDY HAS INCREASED AMERICAN TROOP STRENGTH IN VIETNAM TO 16,000 ADVISERS ...

Kennedy also sent bright young people overseas for other reasons; his Peace Corps attracted over 7,000 idealistic volunteers in its first two years.

In the 1960s, perhaps the most effective American aid program ever began to bear fruit: the "Green Revolution." Beginning in 1944, the agronomist Norman Borlaug developed higher-yield grain cultivars that helped make Mexico self-sufficient in wheat by 1963, Pakistan likewise by 1968, and India self-sufficient in all cereals by 1974. Worldwide, the "Green Revolution" may have saved over a billion people from starvation.

WE WILL BE GUILTY OF CRIMINAL NEGLIGENCE, WITHOUT EXTENUATION, IF WE PERMIT FUTURE FAMINES.

Congress was writing a lot of blank checks then. Using his three decades of legislative experience to good effect, Johnson pushed through a series of bills he hoped would build the "Great Society."

IT'S ALL AMMO FOR THE *WAR ON POVERTY*.

I HOPE IT GOES AS WELL AS YOUR OTHER WAR.

MASS TRANSIT ACT

CHILD SAFETY ACT

ENDANGERED SPECIES ACT

NATIONAL ENDOWMENT FOR THE ARTS

FOOD STAMPS

ELEMENTARY AND SECONDARY EDUCATION ACT

HEAD START

WATER QUALITY ACT

MEDICAID

MEDICARE

Johnson's Civil Rights Act of 1964 also banned employment discrimination against women, who went from 33% of the workforce in 1950 to 43% in 1970.

Johnson reopened the golden door with the Hart-Celler Act of 1965, which abolished the restrictive national quota system and allowed unlimited "family reunification." Within 20 years, annual immigration totals more than doubled. Immigrants increasingly came from Asia, Latin America, and the Caribbean rather than Europe.

ADOBO

ROPA VIEJA

PIEROGI

BURRITOS

PHO

NAAN

The 1960s (and 1970s) saw the biggest youth movements since the 1820s (and 1830s). The median age actually dropped from 29.5 in 1960 to 28 in 1970. The 76 million kids born between 1946 and 1964 made up a "Baby Boom" of epic proportions. The birth control pill, approved in 1960, ended the Boom …

… and brought the "sexual revolution" to the Boomers.

GIRLS SAY YES TO GUYS WHO SAY **NO**

Rock and roll shortened its name to "rock," and got all serious.

Drug use blossomed; LSD moved from psychiatry to the counterculture, and marijuana use likely increased by 1000% from 1962 to 1967.

EIGHT MILES HIGH AND WHEN YOU TOUCH DOWN YOU'LL FIND THAT IT'S STRANGER THAN KNOWN

Youth politics radicalized – on all sides.

WALLACE '68

In 1967, 100,000 young people swarmed into San Francisco for the "Summer of Love," which broadcast – and marketed – the hippie lifestyle to all America.

The Sixties climaxed with the music festival at Woodstock, New York in August of 1969, and ended with a fatal stabbing at the Altamont Music Festival four months later.

AFTER ALL, WHEN THE LAST BABY BOOM TOOK OVER, EVERYTHING WORKED OUT.

DON'T TRUST ANYONE BORN AFTER 1830!

After three years of increasing agitation, the Twenty-sixth Amendment was ratified in 1971, lowering the national voting age to 18.

Not all of Johnson's wars went astray. In April 1965, he landed marines in the Dominican Republic to bolster the anti-socialist side in a burgeoning civil war. Seventeen months (and 13 American fatalities) later, the Americans withdrew, leaving behind a stable right-wing government.

I SAY AGAIN, I SEE NO PIGS. NO PIGS IN THIS BAY.

Anti-war protest hit the big time in 1967, with 400,000 people marching in New York City in August and 100,000 in Washington in October. Regardless, "hawks" outnumbered "doves" in a Gallup poll that winter, 52% to 35%.

DEMON, COME OUT!

IÄ! YOG-SOHOTH!

U.S. PENTAGON

Rising inflation and black unemployment, along with misguided "urban renewal" and white police brutality, contributed to a string of race riots from Rochester in 1964 (4 dead, 350 injured) and Watts in 1965 (34 dead, 1,072 injured) to Newark (26 dead, 725 injured) and Detroit (43 dead, 467 injured) in 1967. Unlike the white-instigated riots of 1919, these often began with black resistance.

BURN, BABY, BURN!!!

LONG HOT SUMMER

In 1968, on Tet (the Vietnamese New Year), cities burned in South Vietnam in a last-ditch Vietcong offensive ending in military disaster. The Vietcong and North Vietnamese army lost 100,000 fighters and retreated into the border zones.

DID YOU HEAR? GENERAL WESTMORELAND SAID "THE ENEMY IS UNABLE TO MOUNT A MAJOR OFFENSIVE."

THAT MUST BE WHY THEY SIMULTANEOUSLY LAUNCHED 114 MINOR OFFENSIVES INSTEAD.

Unfortunately, General William Westmoreland's unwarranted optimism and McNamara's incrementalism had eroded both the media's and the public's faith in Johnson's war. Tet was a victory too late; the President dropped out of the 1968 campaign in March.

TO SAY THAT WE ARE CLOSER TO VICTORY TODAY IS TO BELIEVE, IN THE FACE OF THE EVIDENCE, THE OPTIMISTS WHO HAVE BEEN WRONG IN THE PAST.

TO SUGGEST WE ARE ON THE EDGE OF DEFEAT IS TO YIELD TO UNREASONABLE PESSIMISM.

TO SAY THAT WE ARE MIRED IN STALEMATE SEEMS THE ONLY REALISTIC, YET UNSATISFACTORY, CONCLUSION.

Coincidentally, that month marked a turning point in another seemingly unending struggle. Cesar Chavez, founder of the United Farm Workers, went on a 28-day hunger strike to draw attention to a grape-pickers' strike that had also ground on since 1965. The growers signed a union contract the next year.

BECAUSE WE HAVE SUFFERED -- AND ARE NOT AFRAID TO SUFFER -- IN ORDER TO SURVIVE, WE ARE READY TO GIVE UP EVERYTHING, EVEN OUR LIVES ...

Chavez' model for political action, Dr. Martin Luther King Jr., went to Memphis, Tennessee, to support another strike, by sanitation workers.

On April 4, 1968, a sniper killed Dr. King there.

When he heard the news, presidential candidate Robert F. Kennedy, campaigning in Indianapolis, gave an impromptu speech to a black audience. Riots erupted in 60 cities across the country – but not in Indianapolis.

LET US DEDICATE OURSELVES TO WHAT THE GREEKS WROTE SO MANY YEARS AGO: TO TAME THE SAVAGENESS OF MAN AND MAKE GENTLE THE LIFE OF THIS WORLD.

LET US DEDICATE OURSELVES TO THAT, AND SAY A PRAYER FOR OUR COUNTRY AND FOR OUR PEOPLE.

On June 5, the night he won the California primary, Kennedy was shot and killed by Sirhan Sirhan, a deranged Palestinian.

The 1968 Democratic National Convention in Chicago wound up nominating Hubert Humphrey amid a "police riot" sparked when the Chicago Police Department clamped down on 10,000 anti-war protesters in Grant Park.

THE WHOLE WORLD IS WATCHING!

AND NOW IT'S GOING TO VOTE REPUBLICAN.

Riots at Columbia, Berkeley, and other universities accomplished little ... except to vault anti-protest politicians like California governor Ronald Reagan into national prominence.

DISSENT MUST STOP SHORT OF INTERFERING WITH THE RIGHTS OF OTHER INDIVIDUALS.

On April 30, 1970, Nixon announced that the United States and South Vietnam were invading Cambodia in order to destroy North Vietnamese supply bases.

THIS IS NOT AN INVASION OF CAMBODIA.

CAMBODIA

The invasion damaged the American war effort more than it did the North Vietnamese: radicals bombed or burned 30 ROTC buildings and campus protest exploded again. At Kent State and Jackson State, National Guard and police fired on protesters, killing six.

Former State Department official Daniel Ellsberg leaked 7,000 pages of top secret Johnson Administration Vietnam documents to the *New York Times;* in a 6-3 decision, the Supreme Court upheld the legality of publishing them.

PENTAGON PAPERS

NO LOOKING!

Other government papers vanished entirely in 1972 when the "national liberationist" American Indian Movement occupied the Bureau of Indian Affairs building in Washington.

HEY, ACCORDING TO THIS, WILLIAM HENRY HARRISON LIED ABOUT HIS BODY COUNTS, TOO!

In 1971 and 1972, Nixon moved to improve relations with the Soviets – the "détente" policy – and with their bitter rivals, the Communist Chinese.

I SEE YOU HAVE KILLED SIX PROTESTERS. ONLY 59,999,994 MORE AND YOU'LL BEAT MY RECORD.

DON'T TEMPT ME.

With Soviet and Chinese aid lessening, North Vietnam gambled on a major invasion of South Vietnam on Easter of 1972; American bombing stopped it dead.

Beginning in November 1974, North Vietnam violated the Paris Peace Accords and invaded the South. Congress refused to provide arms or aid to South Vietnam.

IT'S SOUTH VIETNAM ... THEY SAY THEY'RE BEING INVADED, AND THEY WANT US TO FULFILL OUR TREATY OBLIGATIONS.

GIVE THEM THE NUMBER FOR THE CHEROKEE NATION AND HANG UP.

The end was predictable. Saigon fell on April 30, 1975; with the evacuation of the U.S. Embassy, the last Americans left Vietnam.

The Communists immediately purged and "re-educated" millions in the South; about half a million died, including about 200,000 "boat people" refugees. From 1978, the United States gave some Vietnamese asylum; 245,000 had reached America by 1980, and another 530,000 by 2000.

President Ford lost a close election in 1976 to Democratic governor Jimmy Carter of Georgia.

THERE IS NO SOVIET DOMINATION OF EASTERN EUROPE AND THERE NEVER WILL BE UNDER A FORD ADMINISTRATION.

THANK YOU, LORD!

Carter began deregulating the airline, trucking, and rail industries. He was less successful at cutting spending.

I DON'T KNOW HOW THEY DO THINGS DOWN IN ATLANTA, MR. PRESIDENT, BUT UP HERE SPENDING GOVERNMENT MONEY KEEPS US IN OFFICE.

NO, THAT'S PRETTY MUCH HOW IT WORKS IN ATLANTA, TOO.

Carter also brokered a peace deal between Egypt and Israel, the 1978 Camp David Accords.

But bad news from the Middle East – the fall of the pro-U.S. Shah of Iran, and the ensuing Iran-Iraq War – nearly tripled oil prices in 1979-80.

JUST BURN STUFF YOU DON'T WANT ANY MORE

ENERGY POLICY SPEECHES

The renewed energy crisis helped drive inflation from under 6% to over 13% during Carter's term, while unemployment stayed high at 7.2% and interest rates topped 21%.

WHAT HAVE YOU GOT FOR ME ON THE ECONOMY?

WE'VE COME UP WITH A CATCHY NAME FOR IT: "STAGFLATION!"

WE DECIDED NOT TO GO WITH "MALAISE PLUS."

After the fallen Shah was admitted into the United States for medical treatment, 400 Iranian "students" seized the U.S. Embassy in Tehran on November 4, 1979, taking 66 hostages (later reduced to 52).

Carter continued Nixon's détente policy, negotiating the SALT II arms limitation treaty with the Soviets in June 1979.

THERE'S NO VERIFICATION CLAUSE IN THIS TREATY.

WELL, THAT'S BECAUSE IT WOULD MAKE THE TREATY HARDER FOR US TO BREAK, YOU SEE?

Six months later, the Soviets invaded Afghanistan, and Carter began to increase defense spending.

PREMIER BREZHNEV, WE'RE GOING TO BE BOYCOTTING GRAIN SALES TO THE SOVIET UNION, AND BOYCOTTING THE MOSCOW OLYMPICS.

THE OFFICIAL GRAIN OF THE MOSCOW OLYMPICS? MR. PREMIER, I DON'T THINK YOU'RE LISTENING...

An attempt to rescue the hostages in Iran ended in a dust storm on April 25, 1980. So, to all intents and purposes, did the Carter presidency.

In 1980, Ronald Reagan swept into office on a Republican wave. It was the first defeat of an elected incumbent president since Herbert Hoover.

IT MIGHT BE WELL IF YOU ASK YOURSELF ARE YOU BETTER OFF THAN YOU WERE FOUR YEARS AGO?

IS IT EASIER FOR YOU TO GO AND BUY THINGS IN THE STORES THAN IT WAS FOUR YEARS AGO?

IS THERE MORE OR LESS UNEMPLOYMENT ... THAN THERE WAS FOUR YEARS AGO?

IS AMERICA AS RESPECTED THROUGHOUT THE WORLD AS IT WAS?

DO YOU FEEL THAT ... WE'RE AS STRONG AS WE WERE FOUR YEARS AGO?

Less than 70 days into his administration, an assassination attempt nearly succeeded in aborting the "Reagan Revolution." Instead, Reagan's wit under stress bought him a longer honeymoon with the American public.

I HOPE YOU'RE REPUBLICANS.

Reagan rapidly quashed an illegal strike by the air traffic controllers' union, PATCO, firing 11,345 strikers and accelerating the marginalization of American unions.

I *TOLD* YOU WE SHOULDN'T HAVE ENDORSED HIM.

Reagan revived JFK's policy of steep tax cuts to stimulate the economy, lowering the top bracket from 70% to 28%. Tax revenues increased, though not as fast as the deficit.

GOVERNMENT'S VIEW OF THE ECONOMY COULD BE SUMMED UP IN A FEW SHORT PHRASES: IF IT MOVES, TAX IT. IF IT KEEPS MOVING, REGULATE IT. AND IF IT STOPS MOVING, SUBSIDIZE IT.

Reagan accelerated Carter's deregulation moves, and supercharged Carter's defense buildup. Real defense spending increased by 50% during his first term.

ONCE YOU BUY THE FIRST THOUSAND, THEY GET REALLY AFFORDABLE.

Another Carter holdover, Federal Reserve Chairman Paul Volcker, spent three years choking off inflation. After a short but deep recession, the economy recovered completely. It more than recovered; the Long Boom that began in 1982 has so far tripled the U.S. economy in real terms with only two brief stalls.

Volcker's restraint may have contributed to the savings and loan crisis, by raising the price of money higher than S&L returns on mortgage loans. Congress drastically loosened regulations in an attempt to save the S&L industry, only to create a $200 billion mess when the S&Ls inevitably failed anyway in the late 1980s.

I KNOW A GUY SAVINGS & LOAN

EIGHT NATION SAVING & LOAN PANCAI HUT

NOT A MAFIA FRONT S&L

In the 1960s and 1970s, lawsuits made institutionalizing the mentally ill more difficult, federal law encouraged deinstitutionalization, and budget-cutters defunded expensive community treatment centers and public housing. This created a "perfect storm" of homelessness in the 1980s, exacerbated by disintegrating families in the inner cities.

IT'S ALL WROTE DOWN IN THE BOOK WE'RE LIVING IN!

WHAT DID HE SAY?

SOMETHING ABOUT UNINTENDED CONSEQUENCES OF WELL-MEANING LEGISLATION CAUSING THE HOMELESSNESS CRISIS.

OH, SO HE'S A NUT, THEN.

During the 1970s and 1980s, the primary consequence of the Nixon and Reagan "war on drugs" was to change drug-smuggling patterns from low-profit, high-volume marijuana to high-profit, low-volume cocaine. Drug use of all kinds increased throughout the era, despite Nancy Reagan's "Just Say No" campaign.

THIS MUST BE THAT "TRICKLE-DOWN ECONOMICS" I'VE HEARD SO MUCH ABOUT.

The emergence of the AIDS plague in the early 1980s radicalized the gay rights community. The activist Gay Men's Health Crisis founded in 1982 split with the militant ACT-UP in 1987, a year in which over 13,000 Americans died of AIDS.

SILENCE = DEATH

By contrast, the women's liberation movement suffered a major setback in 1982, when the Equal Rights Amendment failed ratification after 10 years.

A WOMAN NEEDS A MAN LIKE A FISH NEEDS A BICYCLE!

BUT THAT SAID, THREE MORE STATE LEGISLATURES WOULD BE NICE!!

A more primitive technology, the truck bomb, destroyed the U.S. Embassy in Beirut on April 18, 1983, and then on October 23, the barracks of U.S. Marines in Lebanon to enforce a ceasefire. 258 Americans died in the two bombings; Reagan withdrew the American presence the next year.

Hezbollah, the Iranian-backed terrorist group responsible, carried out an ongoing campaign of kidnapping hostages as insurance against retaliation. From 1982 to 1988, Hezbollah took 25 Americans hostage; 10 were killed or died in captivity.

On October 25, 1983, Reagan took advantage of a coup on the Cuban-allied island of Grenada to invade the island and install a friendly democratic government. U.S. forces had more trouble staying out of each other's way than they did with the Cubans.

GOSH, I HOPE WE'LL ALL FIT.

GRENADA

Reagan also hugely expanded the Carter program of aid to the anti-Soviet mujahideen rebels in Afghanistan, from $20 million in 1980 to $630 million in 1987.

WHAT'S RUSSIAN FOR "VIETNAM," MAHMOUD?

The "Reagan Doctrine" covered more than Afghanistan. The United States provided covert aid to anti-Communist forces in Angola, Cambodia, and Nicaragua, and supported the anti-Communist government in the El Salvador civil war.

IT'S LIKE IT'S NOT SAFE TO INVADE PLACES ANY MORE.

Reagan didn't neglect Europe, either. Despite immense protests, the United States and NATO deployed advanced Pershing II and cruise missiles in Germany, Italy, and Britain, countering Soviet SS-20s and leveling the apocalyptic playing field once more.

NO WAR!

Mashine Brennt!

Hinter Uns Die Sinflut

Zuviel Hitze!

Rising prosperity and new Cold War toughness carried Reagan to a landslide re-election victory in 1984, carrying every state except Minnesota.

IT'S MORNING AGAIN IN AMERICA, AND UNDER THE LEADERSHIP OF PRESIDENT REAGAN, OUR COUNTRY IS PROUDER AND STRONGER AND BETTER. WHY WOULD WE EVER WANT TO RETURN TO WHERE WE WERE LESS THAN FOUR SHORT YEARS AGO?

Reagan's second term moved toward a post-Cold War world. In the Philippines, South Korea, and Chile, the United States backed democratic movements and encouraged the ouster of anti-American dictators.

MINE SAYS "GOOD LUCK …

… ON YOUR RETIREMENT."

MINE, TOO.

The tenth mission of *Challenger*, the second space shuttle, started on January 28, 1986. It stopped 73 seconds afterward.

So did America.

During 1986, Reagan signed three major laws. The Goldwater-Nichols Act finally streamlined the U.S. military chain of command, mandating full cooperation between the various services to avoid near-fiascos like Grenada.

The Tax Reform Act flattened taxes still further, while closing loopholes and tax shelters.

I DON'T THINK THIS LAND IS WORTH ANYTHING WITHOUT A TAX SHELTER ON IT … WHERE CAN I UNLOAD IT?

TRY A SAVINGS AND LOAN … THEY'RE BACK ON PAGE *172*.

The Immigration Reform and Control Act stiffened the laws on undocumented workers … but provided an amnesty (and eventual citizenship) for 2.1 million undocumented workers, mostly Mexican.

I THINK CONGRESS IS SCHIZOPHRENIC OR SOMETHING.

WELCOME TO LIFE AS AN AMERICAN, JOSE.

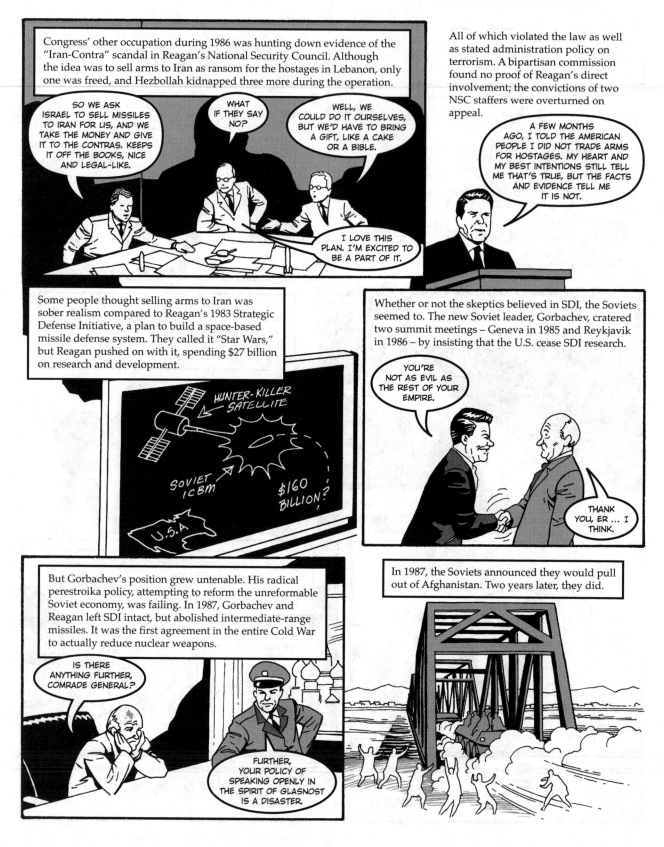

Congress' other occupation during 1986 was hunting down evidence of the "Iran-Contra" scandal in Reagan's National Security Council. Although the idea was to sell arms to Iran as ransom for the hostages in Lebanon, only one was freed, and Hezbollah kidnapped three more during the operation.

SO WE ASK ISRAEL TO SELL MISSILES TO IRAN FOR US, AND WE TAKE THE MONEY AND GIVE IT TO THE CONTRAS. KEEPS IT OFF THE BOOKS, NICE AND LEGAL-LIKE.

WHAT IF THEY SAY NO?

WELL, WE COULD DO IT OURSELVES, BUT WE'D HAVE TO BRING A GIFT, LIKE A CAKE OR A BIBLE.

I LOVE THIS PLAN. I'M EXCITED TO BE A PART OF IT.

All of which violated the law as well as stated administration policy on terrorism. A bipartisan commission found no proof of Reagan's direct involvement; the convictions of two NSC staffers were overturned on appeal.

A FEW MONTHS AGO, I TOLD THE AMERICAN PEOPLE I DID NOT TRADE ARMS FOR HOSTAGES. MY HEART AND MY BEST INTENTIONS STILL TELL ME THAT'S TRUE, BUT THE FACTS AND EVIDENCE TELL ME IT IS NOT.

Some people thought selling arms to Iran was sober realism compared to Reagan's 1983 Strategic Defense Initiative, a plan to build a space-based missile defense system. They called it "Star Wars," but Reagan pushed on with it, spending $27 billion on research and development.

HUNTER-KILLER SATELLITE

SOVIET ICBM

$160 BILLION?

U.S.A

Whether or not the skeptics believed in SDI, the Soviets seemed to. The new Soviet leader, Gorbachev, cratered two summit meetings – Geneva in 1985 and Reykjavik in 1986 – by insisting that the U.S. cease SDI research.

YOU'RE NOT AS EVIL AS THE REST OF YOUR EMPIRE.

THANK YOU, ER ... I THINK.

But Gorbachev's position grew untenable. His radical perestroika policy, attempting to reform the unreformable Soviet economy, was failing. In 1987, Gorbachev and Reagan left SDI intact, but abolished intermediate-range missiles. It was the first agreement in the entire Cold War to actually reduce nuclear weapons.

IS THERE ANYTHING FURTHER, COMRADE GENERAL?

FURTHER, YOUR POLICY OF SPEAKING OPENLY IN THE SPIRIT OF GLASNOST IS A DISASTER.

In 1987, the Soviets announced they would pull out of Afghanistan. Two years later, they did.

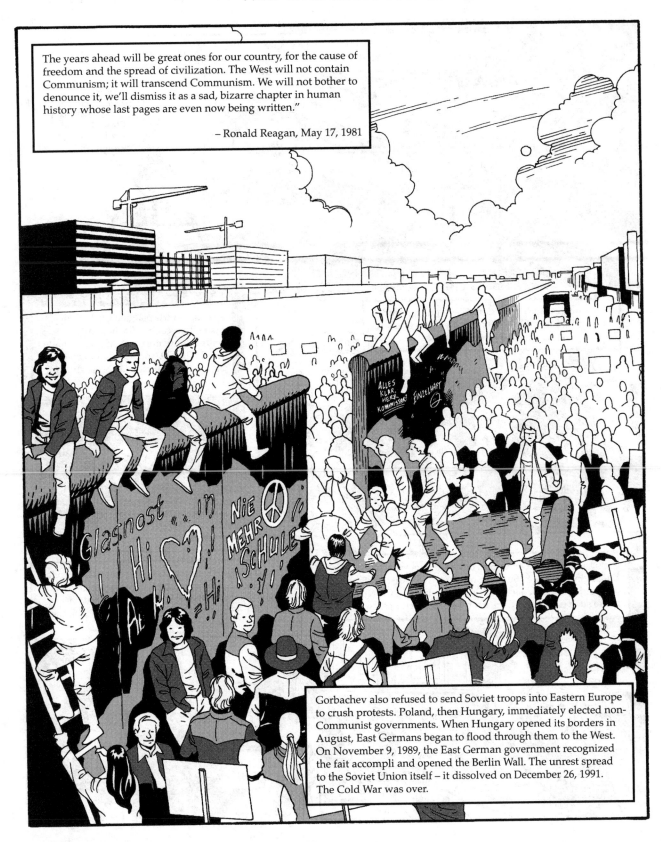

But most of Bush's attention was overseas, and not just on the disintegrating Soviet empire. In December of 1989, U.S. troops invaded Panama to depose its dictator, Manuel Noriega, who took refuge in the Vatican Embassy.

I'LL COME OUT IF YOU'LL JUST PLAY SOME CLAPTON.

In August 1990, Iraqi dictator Saddam Hussein conquered his neighbor Kuwait, eventually triggering a U.S.-led retaliatory air attack and invasion under UN auspices.

HOOAH! IT'S JUST LIKE THE KOREAN WAR ALL OVER AGAIN!

UM...

Beginning the ground campaign on February 24, 1991, the United States liberated Kuwait in 100 hours, but did not move deeper into Iraq to overthrow Saddam. Instead, CIA broadcasts urged Iraq's oppressed minorities to revolt.

... URGE ALL IRAQIS TO RISE UP AGAINST THE BA'ATH PARTY AND SADDAM HUSSEIN ...

HUZZAH! THE AMERICANS WILL FREE US FROM SADDAM'S TYRANNY!

LET'S SEE IF WE CAN GET HUNGARY OR SOUTH VIETNAM ON THIS RADIO FIRST ...

When the Kurds and Shiites did so, Saddam's forces killed tens of thousands of them. Although Bush did not intervene in the rebellion, he did eventually impose "no-fly zones" which stabilized the situation and allowed an independent Kurdish region to flourish.

TANKS ONLY, DOWN THERE! TANKS ONLY!

In December 1992, President Bush deployed American troops to safeguard a UN famine-relief mission in Somalia. On October 3, 1993, 18 American soldiers died in a massive street battle in Mogadishu; the new president withdrew American forces the next year.

But by then the economy had come out of the 1991 recession. One impetus was the creation of the World Wide Web by a European team – and the introduction in 1993 of the first popular graphical web browser, Mosaic, by Marc Andreesen at the University of Illinois.

Once anyone could find the Web, Americans found money in it. In just five years, the Internet economy in the United States was over $300 billion, employing 1.2 million Americans. It was the economic equivalent of creating the entire U.S. automotive industry in five years, without the pollution.

YOU ORDERED A NEW ECONOMY ONLINE, RIGHT? SIGN HERE.

On April 19, 1995, a paranoid former security guard named Timothy McVeigh detonated a truck bomb at a federal office building in Oklahoma City, killing 168 people. The Clinton administration responded with a major FBI operation against right-wing "militia movements" in the U.S.

The Soviet collapse triggered a similar collapse in Yugoslavia in 1991. In 1995, the United States led NATO in a series of air strikes on Serbian forces in Bosnia to force a peace. Clinton sent U.S. troops into Bosnia after the accords as peacekeepers.

THIS CAN'T END WELL.

In 1996, Republicans in Congress and Clinton passed a welfare reform act tying welfare benefits to work. Welfare case loads dropped sharply afterward, as did child poverty.

Al-Qaeda attacked America again on August 7, 1998. Two simultaneous car bombs damaged the U.S. Embassies in Kenya and Tanzania, killing 233 people, including 12 Americans.

But more important things were happening in Washington! In 1998, President Clinton committed perjury in a sexual harassment suit, and the Republican House decided to impeach him for it. The Republican Senate voted to find him not guilty, and Clinton's job approval ratings rose despite the whole debacle.

I DID NOT HAVE SEXUAL RELATIONS WITH THAT WOMAN.

IT DEPENDS ON WHAT THE MEANING OF THE WORD "IS" ... IS.

WHAT WAS THE QUESTION AGAIN?

In 1999, the Yugoslavian war had spread into Serbia itself. Again, the United States led NATO air attacks, this time against Serbia, to safeguard the minority Muslim Kosovar population. After 80 days, the Serbs again backed down, and U.S. troops joined the UN peacekeeping force in Kosovo.

SERIOUSLY, WHAT PART OF "OVERWHELMING AIR SUPERIORITY" DO YOU PEOPLE NOT UNDERSTAND?

On October 12, 2000, al-Qaeda suicide bombers struck the *USS Cole* in the port of Aden, killing 17 American sailors.

In 2000, Clinton's vice president, Al Gore, ran against the Republican governor of Texas (and son of the previous President Bush), George W. Bush. The hard-fought election came down to Florida's electoral votes, though Gore won the popular vote.

A series of recounts and lawsuits mounted up until the Supreme Court ruled 5-4 that Florida's recount was not only unconstitutional but irreparable. George W. Bush thus won the narrowest Presidential election victory in American history.

BY A VOTE OF 5-4, THIS COURT RULES THAT THE PRESIDENT-ELECT OF THE UNITED STATES IS ... *SAMUEL J. TILDEN.*

On September 11, 2001, al-Qaeda terrorists hijacked four U.S. airliners, piloting two into the World Trade Center and one into the Pentagon. On the fourth airliner, the passengers fought back, crashing the plane in Pennsylvania before the terrorists could destroy the U.S. Capitol Building. The attacks killed 2,974 people, and 24 remain missing.

Index